Fear took away from me what I loved most - riding horses. I felt desperate and alone. Nobody understood, not even me. How could I have so totally lost confidence – and how could I get it back? Horse books, trainers, and riding instructors offered great advice, but nobody could tell me "how" to eradicate fear. Fearless people cannot understand the paralyzing effect of unreasonable fear.

I needed someone who truly knew the grip of fear to help me. I needed someone like me, with a fear so intense, that even the most kid-broke, bombproof horse would become a quivering ball of nerves with me in the saddle. Most people with my level of fear simply quit riding. I was almost ready to admit defeat and hang up my saddle – then a tiny clue came to mind and I decided to give it one last shot.

It was clear that a bombproof horse would not eradicate my fear. The problem was not the horse, it was me. I had to become a bombproof human!

While examining fear, readers journey with me into the world of horse as my equine experience began and almost ended.

The pieces finally came together - the puzzle made sense. I'm back in the saddle! As a bombproof rider, I put a smile on my horse's face - and I want to put a smile on your face as you too become a bombproof human.

Donna

☺

Part I - Entering the Horse World

Part II – Looking For a Miracle

Part III – Becoming Bombproof

Part I - Entering the Horse World

"Wow! I'm riding a horse!" Realizing my childhood
dream of riding horseback made me feel
as though I could accomplish anything!

Chapter 1 - Fort Lost-In-The-Woods

"You wouldn't believe this place, mom. They call it

Fort Lost-in-the-Woods because it is in the middle of

nowhere."

Talking to my mother on the phone was a luxury that

hadn't happened very often during the four years we had

lived in West Germany. In the 1980's, before computer and cell phones, phone calls home to the United States were expensive

"Missouri is hot and humid, there's barely room for all six of us inside the cabin where the air conditioning makes breathing possible, and there is a hairy brown creature under the porch. It's bigger than the poodle and fearless. It doesn't run away when I let the dogs out!"

Two kids, two dogs and two adults were crammed into a tiny one-bedroom cabin on a wooded hillside of our new military home, Fort Leonard Wood, Missouri. The cabin, one of the few units of temporary housing where pets were allowed, became home for a month while we house-hunted and waited for our household goods to arrive from overseas.

My husband was in-processing and the kids had walked down the hill to the Shoppette convenience store with quarters in their pockets. I seized the opportunity to call my mom.

Mom reminded me that I was the original nature girl

4

who would rather be outdoors doing guy things than sewing, cooking or cleaning. It was true, as a kid I preferred to mow the lawn, fix a bike, take out the trash--anything to be outdoors.

My childhood home was located on the edge of a small mining town in Northern Minnesota. I spent happy hours galloping through the woods on imaginary horses and setting up camps where I pretended to live with my animals.

Nature and animals were my passion. I dreamed of becoming a veterinarian so I could be around animals all the time - horses in particular. While girls my age were playing with dolls and having tea parties, I was out grubbing in the dirt building miniature farms for my favorite toys, plastic horses. I created elaborate corrals and barns to stable my herd that measured three inches at the withers.

When I was five, I was given a beagle puppy for Christmas, but when my baby sister was born with severe allergies the puppy had to go.

Fourth of July celebrations in our small town involved

parades and pony rides. My dad would let me ride the ponies and then hurry me into the basement of our house where my clothes were immediately washed and I was run through the shower to avoid aggravating my little sister's eczema.

Reading about animals made up for not being able to have real animals. Horse books were my favorite. Even fictional stories were loaded with facts about horses, facts that I carefully stored away for future reference.

"You're right, mom," I replied, feeling sheepish to have complained about life in a cabin in the woods, something I dreamed of as a child, "But don't forget that this nature girl hates bugs, and there are some awfully mean ticks here!"

I shuddered, remembering the walk I had taken the day before in the woods. When I returned to the cabin, my ankles looked like they were filthy with dirt. Upon closer examination I was horrified to realize that the little specks of dirt were actually hungry seed ticks the size of a pin head happily latched onto my skin for a meal.

"Living in the Missouri woods is not like being in Minnesota. It is seriously hot and humid, the dogs could get eaten, there are millions of micro-ticks and..."

Mom interrupted, "When you wrote me from Germany about your move, didn't you say that there was supposed to be a horse stable at Ft. Leonard Wood?"

That was just like Mom to knock the wind out of my-self pity. She knew the mention of horses would divert my attention from something I feared to something I loved.

"That's a good idea, Mom. We need to find the horse stable. Maybe it won't be so bad here if I can see a real live horse up close."

After hanging up the phone I smeared calamine lotion on my itching ankles, locked the dogs inside the cool cabin, safely away from groundhogs, grabbed the Fort Leonard Wood map and walked down the hill to find Andy and Amy.

"Hey kids let's walk to the horse stable."

A huge red indoor riding arena stood at the entrance

7

of the stable complex. The Riding Academy office was built on the front end of a long ancient-looking wooden structure. Inside were 30-some tie-stalls flanking each side of a concrete center aisle. Horses wearing saddles stood in some of the stalls, facing the aisle way watching people busily doing horse-related tasks.

"Kin I help ya?" asked a tall skinny grey haired man wearing a short sleeved shirt fastened with snaps instead of buttons.

"I…uh…we'd like to look at the horses…if it is okay." I stammered, feeling overwhelmed by being so close to the tail-swishing objects of my fondest childhood dreams.

"Sure can. Ya gonna ride today too? We got a trail going out in 'bout 15 minutes." the man drawled in a local Ozark dialect.

Amy's eyes lit up. "Can we mom? Pleeease….."

Amy was as horse-crazy a kid as I had been. Her prize collection of My Little Ponies" was reaching about a hundred head.

I answered the man, "Um...well, you see, we've never ridden before, so I don't know...." I looked at the kids wondering if we would be able to control 1000 pounds of horse without ever having had riding lessons.

"That ain't no problem, ma'am. We dun got gentle horses for ya greenhorns, an' we send ya out with a guide. We'll tell ya how to ride, an' the horses will teach ya too. You 'n the young 'uns will git along jist fine. "

We were assigned horses and instructed on how to lead them across the road to a grassy area where the riding trail began. I had read hundreds of books describing how to mount and ride a horse but my mind was a blur. Thankful for step-by-step instructions, I put my left foot in the stirrup and swung my leg over the saddle of Peaches, a white horse covered with tiny red speckles.

As I settled into the saddle I felt a rush of fear. Ever since I kindergarten I'd been terrified of heights. The indoor slide in the kindergarten classroom was, in my opinion, a structure of torture. Halfway up the ladder on my first day of

9

class, I froze and had to be extracted by my teacher who suggested that I play in the sandbox instead.

Standing on a low stepstool as an adult brought the icy grip of panic, and here I was sitting on a horse at least five feet above the ground. My mouth went dry and I felt the color drain from my face.

"Ya okay there Blondie? I heard the grey-haired stable manager ask me.

"Not really. Heights scare me." I drew in a breath and added, "A lot."

My twelve-year-old son, Andy, encouraged, "Come on, Mom. You can do it. This will be fun!" He was mounted on a light golden palomino named Governor.

"Ya, mom." Chimed in ten-year-old Amy, from the back of a creamy yellow horse whom she patted affectionately. "Fred is ready to go. You can do it mom!"

I ran my tongue over my parched lips, wondering where my spit goes when I'm afraid, and said "Okay, I'll try. Let's ride."

Turning my frightened focus away from the ground helped. When I looked between Peaches' ears to the trail ahead I felt better. I was on a horse finally--at age 36 my dream was coming true. I was riding a real live horse through the woods!

Andy and Amy were riding ahead single file following the trail guide and a few other guest riders. They looked natural and relaxed on their horses.

Halfway through the ride I became more accustomed to my position above ground and began to feel confidence. The horses had spread out and we could barely see the rider immediately ahead of us as the trail snaked through lush green trees.

Quartz laden rocks along the trail sparkled like diamonds in the sun. Thoroughly enjoying the ride, I was lost in thought about the "how-to's" I had read over the years. So this is what it feels like, neck reining, moving "with" the horse, toes up heels down.

A sudden yelp from Amy brought my attention back to

the present. Her horse Fred had taken a short cut ducking under a low hanging branch leaving Amy hanging by her belly on the tree.

Trying not to laugh, I instructed her, "Wait there. I'll be right back!"

I hurried Peaches so I could grab hold of Fred's reins before he disappeared down the trail. With Fred in tow, I returned to the tree to help Amy down.

"That's not funny, Mom." Said Amy pretending to pout. "You laughed at me stuck up in that tree, and then I thought you were riding away and leaving me hanging there."

"Quit complaining. You climb trees like a cat." I said with a grin. "Now, we have to get back up on these horses so we can catch up with the others. I'm sure we can't get lost. I've read that horses never forget where their supper is located, but I'd rather not take a chance."

My book-learning was put to the test. I held two horses still while helping Amy climb back up on Fred and then I mounted Peaches. Awesome! I did it!

"You ready? Now we're going to have to hurry to catch up!" I told her.

With a grin, Amy kicked Fred and said "Okay, let's go!"

I followed on Peaches, one hand on the reins and one hand clamped onto the saddle horn to try and hold my butt still in the saddle as our horses moved into a bone-jarring trot.

When we caught up with the rest of the trail ride and slowed Peaches and Fred to a walk, Amy said, "That was fun!"

From that moment Amy and I were hooked. Two horse-crazy kids were realizing their dreams and entering the world of horse.

Amy and Fred

Chapter 2- Learning to Ride

Learning to ride was a combination of asking questions, remembering what I had read, and applying it all to what I was experiencing. I was learning a seat-of-the pants method of riding. As my ability to control horses improved, I was allowed free rides in exchange for leading trails. Amy was too young to lead trails, but happily rode drag for me. As the last rider in the group, she was able to keep an eye on insecure riders and call out instructions to people if they needed help.

My favorite stable horse was Texas Red, a dark sorrel who bucked when he was crowded by a horse from behind and was afraid of being tied.

Texas Red won my heart one day when I was asked to lead just one man on a trail ride. I had a gut feeling that something was not quite right about that ride. Sure enough, halfway through the ride, the guy said his saddle was slipping. The saddle looked fine to me, but I stopped Texas Red to check the girth anyway. The guy quickly dismounted and when I stepped to the cinch side of his saddle, he grabbed my arm and proceeded to make amorous advances towards me. Texas Red, apparently sensing my alarm, snorted and pushed himself between myself and the offender, giving me time to quickly mount and leave the man to find his own way back to the barn.

The look on the stable manager's face when I rode in on Tex alone told the story - I had been set up for one of the manager's buddies to "get a little." The joke was on him thanks to my protector, Texas Red. From that point on I made it clear that my goal was to learn to ride and care for horses. Period. I wasn't interested in playing games or exchanging sex for favors. I wanted to work hard and become adept at caring for and riding horses.

My persistence paid off. That winter I was allowed to adopt two Academy horses and care for them during the off-season as though they were mine. I chose a sorrel with a long flaxen mane named Skeeter for Amy, and Texas Red for myself. I felt as though I were enrolling in a winter quarter of "Horse Care 101."

Amy was in school so she was able to ride only on weekends, but I rode every day whether it was sunny or snowing. When I discovered that sitting directly on Texas Red's back kept me warm in cold weather, I dispensed with a saddle and began riding with a bareback-bronc-bucking rigging. The 'bronc-rig,' as I called it, helped me mount and provided an emergency handle.

I prided myself on my growing ability to ride at a trot or lope and even jump logs without holding onto the handle. As my ability to ride increased, so did my self confidence. I felt that I could accomplish things in life, and that I could stand on my own two feet.

My growing feeling of self esteem and "can do" attitude was not well received by my husband. For fifteen years I had been an army wife, living in his shadow, dependent upon him for everything. As an officer, he was used to being in charge and I believed it was my duty to follow unquestioningly.

Horses began showing me that I had abilities and self worth. I watched Amy blossom and gain confidence in much the same way. Horses were helping her develop self esteem and responsibility.

The riding stable horses would be our buddies forever, but I felt an instinctive need to buy our very own horses.

My first horse, Skipper, was a dark sorrel like Texas Red. A five-year-old, he was well broke and well mannered. For Amy I found a 12-year-old light sorrel, the same color as her favorite stable horse, Skeeter. Amy named him Lightning. Andy wasn't as totally horse crazy as Amy and I, and was content to occasionally ride Governor, his favorite stable horse.

I took a part time job as a photojournalist for the local newspaper to pay for my growing horse habit. My husband liked the fact that as the newspaper photographer in the community I was involved with important events and was known by important people. He was not thrilled, however, when I joined the fire department and was sent to fire school so I could get photos of fires from inside burning buildings at all hours of the day or night.

Horses gave me motivation and confidence to develop my personal skills and independence. My husband resented my horses and my fire department involvement. Where I had once accepted my husband's total absorption with the military world, I stopped waiting for bits of his attention. Horses and photography were opening the world up to me. I was becoming a better mom and a stronger person.

Andy mounting Governor

Chapter 3 - Old Trails to New Pastures

Wonderful as the Riding Academy had been at first, it became clear that I had to find a new home for Skipper and Lightning. The stable manager, whom I thought was all talk when he bragged about his many affairs and how women allegedly couldn't keep their hands off of him, decided that he wouldn't stand for my "rejection" any longer.

As a summer recreation aide, hired to lead trails and help care for the Academy horses, the stable manager became my direct boss.

Once I was an employee under his supervision, his flirtatiousness changed into persistence and then to insistence. He took my avoidance of his advances personally. I became a goal - a challenge. He was angry that I would deny him access to my body. One day he pinned me down and tried to force me to have sex with him. I fought hard and made it clear that I did not want any part of such activity.

He began assigning me undesirable tasks, heavy work, and wouldn't allow me to lead trails with my beloved Texas Red. He forced me to lead trails mounted on Rufas, a horse that easily became rattled and hyper. I felt that inexperienced riders were being jeopardized by my leading trails on an unpredictable horse. The manager himself was the one who taught me that some horses were 'bombproof' and reliable in the lead, and others were better left to following the trail ride 'herd.' Rufas lacked the confidence to be a good lead horse.

Finally I was pushed past my limit. I went to the recreation program director and described the stable manager's actions and treatment of me - his trying to wear me down and make me give in to him. My idyllic horse world was being turned upside down. I was disillusioned and an emotional wreck.

The ensuing investigation was decided in my favor. My summer-hire position was extended an extra month to make it clear that I was not being retaliated against, and the stable manager was reprimanded and re-educated on sexual harassment issues.

Despite the victory, and partly because of it, I felt it was safer to move our horses from the riding academy. Amy was growing up, and I didn't want her to be in an environment where she could one day be viewed as a sexual plaything.

Jack and Nancy Laurie had just moved into the area and were starting up a boarding facility. As their first boarder I worked off the fees by picking manure out of a designated number of stalls each day and helping with evening feedings.

Amy began having trouble with Lightning. He had been as thin as a rail when I bought him, and lacking energy, he was docile and compliant. When he reached his correct weight, holes in his training and serious bad habits began showing. The move to the new stable intensified Lightning's negative behavior.

He would rear up in objection to being asked to ride out without another horse along. I learned to smack him on the butt with a stick and make him move forward, but Amy was becoming afraid to ride him.

Jack took me aside one day and said, "Lightning's going to ruin your daughter's ability to ride. She's losing her confidence. I've got a big blue-eyed pony due to come to the barn soon. She's badly overweight and needs fine tuning. Why don't you work with the pony for me, ride her, and see what you think. It may be a good horse for your daughter." We could work out a trade.

Lady Blue Eyes, while technically just within pony size limits, was big enough for me to enjoy riding. She had a hackney-type trot which was pretty rough to sit, but which ate the ground. I began riding Lady Blue Eyes and under

Nancy's careful instruction began preparing her for pony pleasure classes. Lady Blue Eyes was fantastic! I knew Amy would love her.

Keeping the pony a secret from Amy was the hard part. I had been making excuses for Amy to stay away from the barn when I knew I would be working with the pony.

When I felt Lady Blue Eyes was ready, I told Amy I wanted her opinion about a horse. I was right - Amy loved Lady immediately and felt comfortable riding her. Amy and I spent many long hours riding together down the road, through fields and woods, me on Skipper and her on Lady Blue Eyes.

After a wonderful year of trail rides and horse shows, we realized that Amy was beginning to outgrow Lady Blue Eyes. I accepted Jack's offer of my shoveling more stalls in exchange for breeding fees. The plan was to breed Lady Blue Eyes to Jack's 15.2 hand stallion and produce a bigger horse for Amy.

At this same time I fell in love with a pregnant

chestnut mare that Jack bought. Her name was Ellie, and she had muscles that wouldn't quit. I envisioned showing her at halter. I sold Skipper to a beginner rider and bought Ellie from Jack. Amy and I both had pregnant mares. Jack always had horses that needed exercising, so Amy and I were able to ride daily even after our mares became mamas.

Lady Blue Eyes gave birth to a bright sorrel filly, in April of 1992. Amy thought long and hard about a name for the baby. Using names of her favorite barn horses Amy came up with, Ima Truly Fancy Lady - Truly, for short.

A month later Ellie gave birth to a little bay filly with a tiny star on her forehead. I named her "Lita." When Lita was weaned, I sold her to a fellow boarder. I had been laid off from my photojournalism job and I was becoming horse-poor.

Jack had many horses and ponies that he didn't have time to train himself and I needed money so I began riding ponies and longing horses for Jack in addition to my stall-cleaning duties. As I learned Jack's method of working with horses he gave me more training projects.

Using Jack's gentle methods of working with foals I taught baby Truly to lead, longe and ground drive. Amy loved to help me work with Truly and could generally be found curled up in Truly's stall holding a long conversation with her equine friend.

"Mom, I want to take Truly for a walk, okay?" I nodded and watched Amy carefully attach a lead line to Truly's halter and head down the driveway to explore the gravel road on foot.

What a great day it would be when Amy would be riding Truly, her pride and joy!

Baby Truly and Amy

Chapter 4 - Shattered

"I'll be overseas for a year." My husband was describing an imminent military assignment, "It will be good, I'll make rank and you will have medical and commissary benefits again."

Military pay and benefits would help the budget immensely. After my husband had voluntarily left active duty for reserve service rather than returning to enlisted ranks when he was passed over a second time for promotion to Major, finances were tight. He had been recalled from reserve military status to an assignment in Honduras, and was excited to be returning to active duty service.

Working with horses was giving me a new self

reliance, and Andy and Amy were dependable, helpful high-school-age kids, so I cheerfully said my goodbyes without any worries or fears.

A month into the school year Amy began having severe pain in her knees and legs. She was experiencing rapid growth and maturation. She lost the look of a little girl and began developing into a full figured woman. Her breasts hurt when she rode, her legs ached, and she began having headaches. Along with physical pain she felt self-conscious about her developing body.

I believed she had issues left over from when her favorite elementary school teacher had committed suicide. Amy at age nine had taken her teacher's death hard. At the time Amy quietly said, "It's okay mom." But I knew it wasn't ok. Amy carried a hurt deep inside.

One morning the cats persistently meowed at Amy's closet door. When I stopped to check out the cats' odd behavior, I heard a sound in the closet. Nobody should have been home. The kids had already left for school - I had watched them walk out the door.

The hair on my neck stood up as I carefully opened the closet door. There sat Amy, hiding and refusing to go to school. It seemed that hurt from the past combined with her growing pains and her new self-consciousness was coming to a head.

I called the Ft. Leonard Wood psychology clinic for an appointment and Amy was seen immediately. In the intake information requested of me, I described Amy's having lost her favorite teacher and my concern that she had been nursing a silent grief for several years. I also noted Amy's self-consciousness and pain involved with her growing body and developing breasts.

At that first visit, I was pressured to give Amy antidepressants. A red flag went up in my mind, and I expressed apprehensions about rushing into drug therapy before even trying counseling.

I was labeled an interfering, overbearing mom who was not letting my daughter grow up. The doctors behind my back told Amy about medicine that would make her feel better - and they told her that I wouldn't let them prescribe it for her. I was the bad guy.

No matter what action I chose, it was going to be wrong. Against my better judgment, I allowed the doctors to prescribe a tricyclic antidepressant, Imiprimine, for Amy. They gave Amy, not me, the prescription form to bring to the military pharmacy. They gave Amy the instructions on dosing. The intent was to put Amy in charge of her own life. My instincts screamed warnings at me, but I dutifully bowed out of their scene and relinquished control to the doctors.

Amy didn't have preliminary blood work done, though she did have an intake EKG. The dosing of the drug was by the book, not tailored to the patient. The changes in Amy were dramatic. She lost weight and her moods would swing from hyper mania to very angry without warning. When the nurses tried to take Amy's vital signs they had trouble finding her pulse. I felt something was seriously wrong, but the doctors weren't talking to me. I was the overly-concerned mom.

Without warning my husband's active duty assignment ended prematurely. He came home and went back on reserve status. The doctors informed me that they were dropping Amy from care immediately because of loss of military benefits.

I begged for an extension of time, as the soonest I could get Amy into a civilian clinic to continue her treatment was two weeks away. The extension was not granted, though I later learned it could and should have been.

Amy had another EKG, was handed two more months worth of the antidepressant, and we were sent home.

Two days later Amy took her life, using the antidepressants I had so distrusted. I found Amy's cold body in her bed on the morning of March 8, 1993. I called 911 while my husband attempted CPR.

Over my fire scanner I heard my fire chief say, "Guys, this is one of our own, it's Photo's daughter." The ambulance and fire rescue arrived. Amy was prepped for transport. It was a scene I was working. It was unreal. Emergencies happen to other people.

I followed the ambulance to the hospital. I could see EMT, Kelly, continuing to perform CPR. Could I have been wrong? Could Amy still be alive?

I don't remember parking my truck. I ran to the Emergency Room door and saw another volunteer firefighter who worked at the hospital running towards me. His face told me what I didn't want to know. I collapsed into his arms and was carried into a conference room.

My emergency scene training kicked in again and I regained my composure. A priest came at my request and gave Amy last rights. My husband arrived and we signed papers. There was a mandatory autopsy, funeral home paperwork, then – the events became a blur.

The next day, after the child protection board had convened, my friends the sheriff and the chief of police both came to my home and said they regretted having to do so, but they had to question me. The military doctors were trying to pin responsibility for Amy's death onto me, the overly concerned mom.

Being falsley accused was like pouring acid into raw wounds. The ensuing investigation proved that the military hospital was negligent in several respects and two years later I settled out of court for cost-of-litigation.

My emotions surged - anger, regret that I didn't listen to my intuition, and fear. Immediately after Amy's death I was overcome with a terror of the dark. It was almost a physical horror to shut my eyes in the shower because it became dark. I felt an overwhelming fear that I was about to be harmed by some invisible force lurking in the darkness.

Later I learned that the mind suffers shock much as our bodies do. For instance, when we donate blood, the sudden loss of blood can produce the effect of physical shock to even the biggest, most burly and brave men. Fainting in the blood donor's chair is a physiological reaction quite beyond a person's control. When a person suffers severe emotional loss, the mind can experience shock and react in very much the same manner. I could no more control the terror of the dark that overcame me than the blood donor could control fainting in response to blood loss.

After a few months, my fear of the dark began to subside, but I had already given up photography as I couldn't bear being in the darkroom to process B&W photos. I stopped going to fires and accident scenes with the fire department.

My husband, who never had felt comfortable dealing with feelings and emotions, was unable to help. I turned to my horses for comfort and stability.

Andy assisted me greatly at this time. I decided to go ahead with the upcoming horse show season and entered Ellie in Western Pleasure and Halter classes. Even though Andy wasn't horse-crazy, he came with me to shows and rode Ellie in Bareback Pleasure classes.

Andy's relaxed riding put Ellie at ease, and they won frequently. Andy and Ellie took a huge year-end trophy. Ellie was stiff and nervous when I rode her in pleasure classes with a saddle. We did okay, but I felt uptight and Ellie mirrored my nervousness.

One day I was working with a pony for Jack in the outdoor arena when I heard a terrible commotion in the barn. I tied the pony and ran to see what had happened. My heart sank as I realized that Ellie had begun to colic again and got herself cast in her stall. This time Ellie was acting differently. She began to sweat and her body temperature went up. By the time the vet arrived she could barely stand on her front feet. Ellie's episode of colic went into full blown founder, a fever condition in her feet which caused severe pain.

The vet tried an experimental procedure of casting Ellie's front feet to try and prevent the coffin bone from separating and rotating downward due to inflammation.

After a week of watching Ellie dealing with utter agony, I made a difficult decision. I gave Ellie to the vet's assistant in hopes that he could care for her beyond what I could afford and hopefully save her life. He tried, but Ellie only lived a couple more weeks.

Truly was two years old and physically ready to start working under saddle. The cartilage in her knee joints was grown over with bone. She could bear the weight of a rider without damaging her legs or back. At 13.2 hands, Truly was registered with the American Quarter Pony Association.

Andy helped me in starting Truly. I felt comfortable riding Truly in the confines of a box stall, so I was the first one on her back, but the thought of riding her in the expanse of the arena frightened me.

Andy's natural calm gave Truly a positive experience during her debut in the arena. I wasn't afraid of falling off of Truly. She was close to the ground, and I had fallen off of many horses and ponies without suffering any damage. I worried that I hadn't instilled enough "brakes" on Truly and that I could have a runaway. I need not have feared. Truly was a perfect lady.

Andy

Andy showing Ellie in bareback pleasure

Chapter 5 - Changes

The first year after losing a loved one to death involves experiencing "firsts" without that person. Loss is felt acutely at special times. My "firsts" were difficult - the first holiday, the first birthday without Amy.

Truly's first birthday was a month after Amy died. Boarders and neighbors came to Jack's barn and we celebrated Truly's birthday with carrot cake and party hats.

The second year of loss is a season of healing. Surviving the hurts of the first year gives strength and encouragement to move on with life. The pain becomes a little easier, and you know you're going to manage. At least that is how it usually is. My husband seemed to be stuck in time. Untouchable emotionally, he became a black cloud of despair. Frightening to me was the onset of his uncharacteristic middle-of-the-night behavior which he didn't remember in the morning.

All I could conclude was that he was either lying, uncharacteristic of him, or that he really didn't know what he was doing at night. Either way, I felt threatened. I realized that if I were going to finish healing and survive Amy's death, I would have to pick myself up and start over on my own. To emerge from the shadows and stand on my own two feet as a whole complete person - I had to get away from the town where I had lost Amy.

While I had many close friends in the town, I hated being there. I felt haunted and anguished, a feeling that persisted every time I had occasion to even drive through the area many years later.

Andy and I both moved away, he to southern Missouri and me to Northern Missouri. I took a job as a greens keeper on a golf course and moved into a mobile home park.

My earthly possessions consisted of Amy's horse, Truly, my truck and a small U-haul trailer loaded with my books, horse tack, clothes, Amy's pony collection, and a few pieces of furniture. The divorce attorney had asked me incredulously, "Is that all you want?" I told him that I just wanted to start over with no debt and make a life for Amy's horse in her memory.

In the mobile home park I met Gary, who I had known back at Ft. Leonard Wood. Gary still lived near Ft. Leonard Wood, but worked during the week at the local state park. He did odd jobs for the mobile home park owner in exchange for a place to live during the work week. With Gary's help I chose a trailer that had a potential for refurbishing.

I found an elderly couple who agreed to board Truly at their farm on the edge of town. My plan was to save as much money as I could and eventually buy my own place in the country where Truly would be able to live in my own back yard.

During the week I felt safe with Gary living close by, but on weekends the trailer park was frightening. It was a haven for substance abusers and workers without green cards. The trailers were crammed closely together and people had little consideration for their neighbors.

Between my job and working to renovate my mobile home, I didn't have much time to ride Truly. Occasionally Gary would borrow a horse and we would ride through town, in parades and through the trails at the state park. To my dismay, I was becoming nervous in the saddle.

I began to worry that I may have missed something in Truly's training and that she would blow up or run off. I wondered if I was losing confidence because I no longer was able to ride daily.

Within three years I had changed jobs several times from mowing golf course greens to operating heavy equipment to construction and I finally landed a job with the State of Missouri. State pay was not very high, but the job had benefits and it was a steady paycheck. It was time to use my savings to get out of the trailer park and move to the country. Once I had Truly in my own care, I could ride her more often and my confidence would return.

Chapter 6 - Beyond My Control

A ten-acre hayfield was advertised for sale at auction. I didn't have the cash in hand needed to purchase real estate but I went to the auction anyway. The land didn't sell that day as the reserve hadn't been met.

I asked Gary if he would come out and look at the piece of land and help me approach the owner with a proposal. In Missouri, I learned, it is wise for a women to have a male negotiating vehicle repairs and any kind of deals involving the exchange of a lot money.

Gary looked at the rolling hills of the hayfield and said, "This is really a nice piece of property. You could put your house right there, and make a walk out basement and..." I looked at him, surprised. I saw a hayfield, Gary saw in his mind's eye the farm, already finished.

Gary became my designer, my foreman, my project

supervisor, and eventually my renter. My house was finished just in time. The trailer park was sold to the school district and trailers were moved out. Gary had nowhere to go, so I began renting to him throughout the week.

Truly lived in my back yard, but I was still too busy to ride her much. There were fences to put up, hay to cut and bale, a barn to build. I enjoyed farm work and I began using it as an excuse to avoid riding.

Then my emotions, which had finally begun healing, suffered another blow. This time it was not personal loss, I was being sexually harassed at work.

Though I voiced my complaint to my supervisor several times, the harassment by a superior continued. He would corner me and expose himself, apparently enjoying my horror. His behavior was becoming bolder and weirder. I feared that his persistent harassment could become a physical attack.

Due to a workplace injury requiring elbow surgery, I was placed on workmen's compensation leave for several months. When my doctor okayed me to return to the workplace, I told him about being sexually harassed and that I was afraid – even more afraid with a weaken arm.

My doctor told me that since I had tried reporting the harassment to my supervisor and nothing was done to protect me, I needed to go to the police. I said that if I involved the police, I'd be fired, to which he replied, "They can't fire you."

As it turned out we were both right.

Far more devastating than the sexual harassment was the retaliation that resulted from my seeking police protection. I was suspended from work for 30 days without pay, my hours were reduced. I was stalked, videotaped and every conversation with my supervisor was secretly tape recorded. I was repeatedly cornered and yelled at by supervisor and the armory commander.

Co-workers were told to either spy on me or avoid me. My workplace became a terrifying place. I applied unsuccessfully for other jobs within the state of Missouri so I wouldn't lose my retirement benefits. I needed my job to keep my farm.

In order to remain financially solvent, I had to simply endure my hostile workplace. Every day when I drove out of the parking lot I cried tears of relief. Having survived another day at work I was heading home to my peaceful haven where I could let my emotional guard down and find healing.

Sharing my farm and the animals in my care has always been a source of enjoyment for me. When some of Gary's family members needed a place to live while moving into the area, my barnyard became a campground.

Two camp trailers became temporary housing. We bought extra horses at a livestock auction and borrowed a kid-broke mare from a friend in order to provide enough mounts for group rides.

While I felt totally comfortable working with horses on the ground, I was dismayed to realize that my riding confidence continued to plummet. What should have been a fun time of riding down the road with other people became a time of torture.

I would sit on Truly's back and pray that whoever was leading the ride wouldn't go faster than a walk. I was at the mercy of the group. If everyone wanted to trot or gallop, I couldn't hold Truly back and was forced to ride faster against my will. I prayed for rain. I avoided riding by mounting other people on Truly and then conveniently running out of horses.

On the rare occasions when I was alone, I would saddle Truly and try to ride her only to be overcome by paralyzing fear. I couldn't define it, couldn't fight it, couldn't understand it - but it was real. I was filled with the same unreasonable fear that overtook me when Amy died, only this time I didn't fear the dark, I feared what I loved most, riding horses.

Horsemanship books teach how to ride, but I couldn't find a book specifically describing how to overcome fear.   I was looking for an elusive miracle.

**Good work, captain – but I'd like
A little more detail in this area**

Chapter 7   Figuring Out Fear

"Donna, put fear into your back pocket and stay on that horse!"

Gary shouted back to me as we were riding home from a local parade.

Despite my pre-parade jitters, riding in the parade had been fun. Truly, seemed to enjoy walking slowly down the street between rows of cheering people. She had been totally calm and I enjoyed myself. When I was a kid I used to love parades where I would have a chance to see and maybe even touch a horse.

Whenever the parade bogged down, I would ride Truly over to kids along the route and let them pat her. Truly approached parade-goers with ears forward, anticipating the possibility of a treat. People loved her.

When we passed by the judges' reviewing stand, the crowd began clapping and cheering. Truly, who had never heard the sound of applause, stiffened and jumped. Her hind feet skittered on the pavement and she did a little dance to regain her balance.

Delighted with Truly's antics, the spectators clapped harder.

I grabbed the saddle horn, tightened my grip on the reins and clamped down on the saddle with my legs. Truly responded with increased power to her hindquarters and began prancing in place. Nostrils flaring, neck arched, Truly was a crowd pleaser. I was terrified. We were well past the reviewing stand but Truly remained excited.

A car door slammed and Truly found motivation to blow. She tried to run but her feet slipped on the pavement and she sat down. After she scrambled back onto her feet I shouted to Gary, "I'm going to lead Truly the rest of the way."

Before I could dismount Gary sternly told me to put my fear in my back pocket and "stay on that horse!"

"He just doesn't know what it's like." I thought angrily. "He's never been paralyzed by fear."

Feeling misunderstood, a surge of anger flooded me and to my surprise overrode my terror. "Okay, damn it, let's go then."

As we headed toward the boarding facility, I consciously fed my anger. Truly was still tense, but her full attention was locked into my anger and she didn't try to spook or run. Riding with the negative emotion of anger was not pleasant, but it served to override fear. Puzzled, but oddly encouraged, I began studying the anger-fear connection.

Anger and fear are opposite emotions, strong reactions to feeling threatened. What a rider feels directly affects the horse. Even a completely "bombproof" horse can blow up in fear if the rider is terrified. I am proof of this. Truly only pranced and became a snorting fearful horse when I was on her back. Other people could ride her with no problem.

Skeeter, the gentle "birthday party horse" at the riding stable was also a horse that anyone could ride. We would mount kids and nervous adults on Skeeter who calmly transported his riders through the hour-long trail rides.

One day, however, Skeeter became totally frazzled and in a blind panic wrapped his rider around a tree before running back to the barn shaking with fear. Afterwards, the lady confessed to having witnessed a horse-wreck involving a big truck several years prior and said she was very nervous about riding. She was apparently so fearful that even stalwart Skeeter couldn't ignore her inner turmoil.

Truly, like Skeeter, has been ridden by novice riders and kids around the arena and down the road without incident. Truly takes good care of her riders but she couldn't deal with my emotions. Deep down I felt out of control and I passed the feeling on to Truly.

I couldn't simply pocket fear as per Gary's instructions. It's not that easy. Fear is unreasonable. A person can look at a non poisonous snake, know that it cannot cause harm, and yet feel panic. Merely thinking, "The snake is harmless - the snake cannot hurt me" doesn't make fear melt away in response to human reasoning ability.

Likewise, sitting on the back of a horse, knowing there is no real danger of falling off, is not enough to banish fear. Telling oneself to be reasonable, does not eliminate panic. Pretending fear is not a factor fails because the harder a person tries to deny fear or reason fear away, the more fear becomes the focus.

When fear is felt, muscles tense up in preparation for flight or fight. Respiration rate increases, salivary glands cease producing spit, digestion stops, thinking becomes altered, and attention is focused on the perceived threat so intently that the rest of the world fades away.

Increased production of sweat is reportedly detected by animals' sensitive olfactory systems. The real culprit though, is the feeling of fear. The slightest bit of human tension is transferred from our butts, thighs and calves to the horse. Tension is also transferred from human hands down the reins into the horse's sensitive mouth where fear signals are received loud and clear. The horse responds to the rider signals with appropriate pre-flight tension - head up, eyes focused, muscles ready to spring into action and flee whatever is upsetting the rider.

The rider in turn senses the horse's nervousness and horse the strong nonverbal cue of imminent danger is passed back and forth between horse and rider like a snowball rolling downhill gaining size and speed.

Often a fearful rider will hunch over in a self-defensive fetal-position posture. The rider's submissive body position thrusts the horse into the leadership role. As the rider loses control, the horse takes over.

Sometimes even when nothing is amiss, a rider will look ahead intently scrutinizing the scene ahead in order to prepare for any potential trouble.

The rider may see a white plastic bag on the ground and remember a past event where a horse spooked at a plastic bag. Memory of the spooking incident draws the past event into the present. The rider's body begins to react to the memory of riding a spooking horse.

The horse senses that something is wrong and follows the rider's visual focus which is relayed by body position. Horse's attention is drawn to the white object. Now both the horse and rider are staring intently at the plastic bag expecting the worst.

Fear is a powerful emotion. Feelings differ from emotions. Feelings are simply responses to our senses as we experience the physical world around us. Emotions are tied to the past and are brought into the present by our thoughts. When we think about the past, our emotional buttons are triggered and the past is dragged into the present.

When the rider's mind flickers to a past event of a horse spooking, it recreates the emotion that accompanied that past event as genuinely as though it were actually happening. The horse doesn't know that the rider's tension is based on a memory, and responds to the rider as though there were something real to fear.

There are many situations in life that can cause

anxiety. Personal loss of control in any life experience is potential fear factor. Loss of control in situations gives a person the feeling of being powerless.

Growing older can bring a feeling of loss of control. Age brings physical changes – stiffness, weight gain, muscle loss, lack of strength and dexterity. Physical fitness can be maintained through exercise and stretching, slowing physical changes, but aging is unavoidable. Caution naturally increases in adult riders. Even rough-and-tumble cowboys tend to stop riding bulls as they grow older. Reaction times slow down. Older bones break more easily and take longer to mend. The ground seems to become harder as people age.

Experiencing or even seeing a horse related accident can shake a person's confidence. The visual image of seeing a wreck or the memory of having fallen off a horse can unexpectedly flood the conscious mind with second-hand, re-lived fear.

Increased knowledge about horses and how they

operate can cause anxiety. Ignorance is bliss. Green riders simply don't know all the "bad" things that can happen. With experience comes a vast memory bank of what can potentially go wrong. Healthy caution can escalate into a fearful projection of negative possibilities.

Murphy's Law in riding: What you think can go wrong, will go wrong. Our fears tend to become realities if we let them. When we first learn to ride we experience new and different sensations of the horse moving underneath us. Without a catalog of accidents and mishaps in our memory banks, we tend to focus on what it feels like to ride a horse right at that moment.

This creates a present-moment partnership with the horse. When learning to ride there may be uncertainties of how to handle a horse or sit to a trot, but novice riders usually are caught up in the newness of the experience and are not worrying about what could possibly go wrong.

We ride with our minds. Negative memories, pressure, worry, feeling inadequate – all these are easily drawn into the present moment when we are riding. When our minds travel to thoughts such as these, we transfer the resulting emotions to the horse.

The Biblical proverb, "As a man thinks in his heart, so is he." can be further stated, "As a person thinks, so is the horse."

Though I couldn't stuff fear in my back pocket and ignore it, and living in anger sounded unpleasant, I hoped that by understanding the role my mind plays in transferring my fear to my horse would help me squelch panic and eliminate fear.

Armed with insight and determination I decided to meet fear head on and find a way back into the saddle. Left foot in the stirrup, I swung my right leg over Truly's back and shoved my right foot into the other stirrup. Truly's ears flickered backwards listening. Even before she heard the tension in my voice as I said, "Easy girl, let's just stand still for a moment," she felt my tension through her saddle and through the reins to the bit in her mouth.

I tried to relax and breathe deeply, A task - I need to do something to take my mind off fear. Before I could think of a drill or task to focus upon, my body gave me away. My breathing became shallow and my hands felt cold and clammy with sweat.

Truly mouthed the bit impatiently and wrinkled her nose. Panic to rise from the pit of my stomach to my head. My hearing dimmed, my vision constricted, my mind locked onto the thought, "My horse wants to go, but what if she spooks? What if I can't hold her back?"

I tried to fight the grip of terror by telling myself, "Put fear into my back pocket. Don't let fear rule me. Relax." But it was no use. I was overpowered by the final big thought, "What if I lose control?"

I slid off Truly's back in tears. What was wrong with me? I used to ride wooded trails, jumping logs and splashing through streams. Now just sitting in the saddle was terrifying.

Shaking with adrenalin I hugged Truly's neck and

apologized. "Sorry girl, it isn't your fault. I just don't know how to not be afraid. You are not the problem. I am. I don't know how yet, but I'll fix it. I promise."

Chapter 8 - Trial and Much Error

Reading self-help books and asking people for their ideas on overcoming fear led me to try a variety of methods.

Get a "Bombproof" Horse

The number one suggestion to overcoming fear of horseback riding is to get a kid-broke, gentle, bombproof horse. Bombproof horses for beginner riders are great, but when an experienced rider loses confidence bombproof horses do not solve the problem.

Horses sense their rider's emotional state and their experience level. When a bombproof horse feels inexperienced hands on the reins a bombproof horse doesn't take the rider's heightened emotion seriously. The bombproof horse overlooks tension and carries the young or green rider safely down the road.

However when the bombproof horse feels the actions and cues of an experienced hand and senses the rider's fear, a red flag goes up in his equine brain. "This person knows the ropes and feels that something is wrong. I better pay attention – there is a threat somewhere."

The experienced rider feels the horse stiffen, and thinks, "This gentle horse is afraid of something!"

Reacting to the horse's tension usually causes an automatic gripping action with the legs hoping to hold on better in case the horse bolts. Gripping and hunkering down into a self-protective position transmits to the horse, "My rider is in jockey position, ready to run!" A frightened inexperienced rider tends to grab the saddle horn. When the experienced rider Instinctively pulls back on reins intending to prevent the horse from running, energy is transferred from horse's front end to the horse's hindquarters. The horse is now in power-gear, hindquarters engaged, totally enabled to run.

The faithful bombproof horse wants to save itself and is willing to save the rider in the process. When an experienced rider senses that the horse is about to blow, fear can cause the rider to quickly dismount. The horse quickly learns that when rider gets off, fear is gone. This breeds a bad habit for both horse and rider.

The problem with fear is not necessarily solved by finding a gentle horse - the problem within the rider, not the horse. Finding a gentle kid-broke horse may help temporarily, but I am living proof that a gentle horse is not always the answer to eradicating fear. My fear caused even gentle kid-broke Truly to act like a skittish green-broke horse.

Pretend You're Not Afraid

Despite my failure to put fear into my back pocket, I felt I had to try again and be more convincing. I tried hard to hide my fear from Truly but the more I tried to "pocket my fear," the stronger my fear seemed to become. I couldn't force myself to relax. The word "force" is opposite of relax. Applying force increases pressure. If I let a water balloon rest in my open palm I can hold onto the balloon easily. If I forcefully try to get a grip on the water balloon I will squeeze the balloon right out of my hand.

If you are told not to think of zebras, the more likely is is that black & white striped creatures will appear in your mind's eye. The harder I tried to deny fear, the more fear became my focus - and my focus became my reality.

Prayer Magic

"Please God take this fear from me." "Please God don't let my horse spook." I used God like a vending machine in the sky. I'd send up desperate prayers hoping for an instant change in myself and my horse. Like a mantra I would quote the Bible verse, "Perfect love casts out fear" followed by, "I love to ride, I love my horse, God your Bible says love casts out fear, so how about casting out my fear?"

Attempting to manipulate God in order to magically change the situation served once again to pin my attention more firmly on fear. Asking God to change my horse was pointless - the problem was not my horse, the problem was me. And even though I loved my horse, God didn't override the situation and magically cast out my fear.

Visualization

Imagination is a powerful tool. Imagining "some beach somewhere" is a great way to manage pain while sitting in the dentist's chair, but when I'm sitting in the saddle I need to be paying attention to what I am doing, not pretending I am somewhere else.

Pre-visualization improved my riding form as I produced the mental image of myself riding with my body positioned correctly, but trying to imagine riding without fear served only to drag fear into the visualization.

Even when I was successful in imagining a picture of myself being totally relaxed in the saddle, in my deepest self

I believed that the picture in my mind was imaginary and that reality would take over when I actually rode.

Visualization can take the edge off of physical pain, hone physical skills and even speed the body's healing process. Shutting my eyes, however, reduced my conscious control of visualization allowing my subconscious mind to run wild with self-defeating images. I had a runaway mind.

Hypnosis

I could not ignore, deny or visualize away the powerful emotion of fear. I thought hypnosis may be a sneaky way to bypass myself and deal the death blow to fear.

During the 1980's I had attended group hypnosis meetings where I practiced the power of suggestion through auto hypnosis for weight loss and stress control. Hypnosis works by putting the conscious mind into neutral by distracting it and then dealing with the subconscious mind.

In searching for updated information on hypnosis, I found an Internet site that offered short streaming video downloads designed to reprogram people's minds regarding how we feel about traumatic events in life, generalized fear, and negative feelings. Some of the streaming videos I found helpful in gaining confidence in the workplace, and for public speaking, but nothing specifically addressed fear of riding horses, so I called the number on the website for assistance specific to my problem with riding horses. The hypnotist was kind, helpful, and very effective. At the end of the telephone induction he said, "Now I don't want to remove all your fear because horses are dangerous animals."

I didn't need that particular reinforcement!

Alcohol or Drugs

Use of mood altering substances takes the edge off reality, slows racing minds and helps humans to not think about all that could go wrong. Alcohol gives a sense of courage by replacing worry with a pleasant feeling of relaxation and of being in control.

When people use chemical courage they feel more in control, but in realty reaction time is impaired. With alcohol or tranquilizers in my system I probably wouldn't transmit tension to my horse. Chemical substances medicate the symptoms of fear, but they don't solve the problem of fear.

While I may not worry so much about falling off, with a slower reaction time I would not be able to accurately ride in sync with the horse. With impaired senses there is a greater chance of having an accident which could ultimately produce even more fear.

Mental focus

I thought back to the past and identified what made me feel the most confident. Focusing on events or tasks, such as riding quickly to rescue someone, concentrating on the patterns of a mounted drill team, or helping round up the neighbor's cattle were times when I was totally comfortable. When my attention was placed on a task, my mind was occupied and I wasn't thinking about fear.

I began to feel a strong hunch that concentrating upon an action instead of imagining what could go wrong could be a way to help me hold fear at bay.

Thomas Edison said that before he succeeded in an invention, he didn't fail, he had simply found many ways that didn't work. Encouraged, I began thinking of things to do while riding in order to keep my mind from running away with me.

Chapter 9 – Saddle Up Anyway

John Wayne said, "Courage is being afraid, but saddling up anyway."

Determined, I began forcing myself to get on Truly and do simple things. Truly developed the bad habit of walking as soon as a rider swung a leg over her back. I focused my efforts on simply mounting and sitting quietly in the saddle with the goal of teaching Truly to stand patiently until receiving the cue to walk. Mounting and sitting in the saddle began gently stretching my stiff riding muscles and gave confidence a starting place.

Putting Truly into motion caused my nervousness to escalate to fear, so I started on a small scale. I rode Truly in small circles in a flat area near my garden with road cones marking an imaginary riding arena.

The boundary of an arena, even an imaginary one, made me feel safer so I bought cattle panels and T-posts and transformed my vegetable garden plot into a makeshift riding arena, a safe-zone in which to battle fear.

I carried horse books and magazines with me and read them in every spare moment, jotting down facts and statements in a notebook. I carefully extracted and compiled helpful riding facts.

A magazine article pointed out that people forget to breathe when afraid. This in turn increases physical tension. I thought back to the first time I rode in a western pleasure class. During my first lap around the show arena, I could hear Nancy Laurie calling to me from the sidelines, "Breathe Donna! Breathe!" I had been nervously holding my breath. Breathing deeply relaxes the physical body.

In his book, *Natural Horsemanship*, Pat Parelli says people must be physically fit, mentally fit, and emotionally fit in order to ride and he says to smile with all four cheeks. I became determined to become fit in all possible ways.

Monty Roberts writes, "You are what you eat" To a horse we smell like meat because we eat meat. I pushed the concept up a level to, "You are what you think." I needed to change my thinking.

My workplace involved much repetitive motion requiring my body but not my brain. While walking briskly or performing rote tasks I began filling my mind with words that described what I wanted to be. I silently thought words like, "confident, competent, peaceful, powerful, patient, kind, strong, flexible, graceful, balanced."

To my positive-words drill, I added body language. I began moving through the day thinking positive words as though they were already descriptive of me. I pulled my shoulders back and held my chin up and put a pleasant expression on my face. I thought of myself as possessing the qualities of the words I was thinking. My body language became a reflection of the qualities I wanted to possess, as though they already existed.

Years of not riding made me feel stiff and

uncomfortable in the saddle. It was difficult to relax with muscles and tendons screaming at me in protest for stretching them beyond their limits. To become more physically fit for riding, I began doing isometric exercise for strength and gentle stretching to increase range of motion in my joints.

My body was becoming more flexible. My attitude was becoming more positive. I began to feel stronger and more able to deal with my workplace. People responded to me differently when I walked with shoulders back, head up and a smile on my face.

When I consistently felt physically more flexible and inwardly more positive, I decided It was arena time. I began riding short 5 to 10 minute sessions. Quality was more important than quantity. Short sessions prevented boredom and kept both Truly and me wanting more.

First I re-taught myself not to look down at Truly as I rode. I had developed the bad habit of watching Truly's head for any warning signs of fear being conveyed by her ears. I also kept an eye on how Truly's body was moving and frequently checked the exact location of the saddle horn – just in case. I forced myself to quit looking for trouble and stop thinking about grabbing leather for security.

Retraining myself to look ahead to where I wanted to go was difficult. Initially I felt as though I were disconnected from Truly. Looking down at Truly and seeing her body movements had given me the illusion of being "with the horse" though the exact opposite was true. Staring down at Truly's body had caused me to ride as a separate entity from her. I had to relearn to ride by feeling and trusting the physical sensation of my body moving in unison with Truly's body.

I made myself look ahead at the arena fence in the direction I wanted to ride and began breathing in sync with Truly's hoof beats. I breathed in slowly and deeply while silently counting, "one, two, three, four, five six" in sync with Truly's steps then breathed out slowly, emptying my lungs, counting, "one, two, three, four, five, six."

While focused on breathing in time with Truly's steps, I began to feel more "with" Truly. Fear melted into the background as I experienced the physical calm that occurs with deep regulated breathing. As a bonus, the deep breathing cleared most of my asthma symptoms.

When Truly began responding to my more relaxed feel in the saddle, I created tasks for us to accomplish.

I began randomly turning Truly in small circles to change directions and increase her flexibility. We made figure eights and practiced the down-and-back maneuvers Jack Laurie had used to train his barrel racing horses. Riding around road cones and stepping over landscape timbers gave us interesting tasks to focus upon.

After many sessions at a walk, I gathered up my courage and asked Truly for a trot. Truly readily stepped into a trot but would not hold the pace. She would trot a quarter of the way around the arena with her head high and then lower her head and return to a walk.

"There are no problem horses, only problem riders." I

quoted to Truly. "What am I doing wrong? "

Truly wrinkled her nose and shook her head.

It dawned on me that my tense body could actually be uncomfortable for Truly. Although I was more relaxed while at a walk, I still had a firm grip on the saddle with my legs and when the pace increased so did my grip.

When Truly began trotting I felt myself clamping so tightly that I worked myself up out of the saddle like squeezing toothpaste out of the tube. I was working against the muscles in Truly's back. I used to pride myself on my ability to sit to a trot without bouncing in the saddle. With Truly's help, and for Truly's sake, I began to teach myself to sit to a trot all over again.

While Truly was standing still I concentrated on melting my butt down into the saddle like a chocolate bar in the sun. I felt my legs melt down the fenders and I let my feet rest lightly on the stirrups.

Taking a deep slow breath I asked Truly to walk. The difference was incredible. Even at a walk I had been sitting like a coiled spring in the saddle. The relaxed feel was more comfortable to me. Surely it would be better for Truly too. Okay, now a gentle squeeze with my calf and "trot."

No luck. Truly started trotting and then quit. Suddenly I realized that while I was saying "trot" with my cues, I was still thinking "Do I really want to do this?" Truly was listening to my innermost mind instead of to my physical cues.

I had to get tough on myself and clearly decide that I wanted to trot. Then I had to be firm with Truly to break her habit of a short obligatory trot before returning to a more comfortable walk. I had to convince Truly and myself, that I wanted to trot and that she would remain in "trot gear" until I cued her to walk.

At first it felt awkward to squeeze with my calves and then nudge Truly with my heels while trying to hold that melted chocolate feeling with my butt and legs.

As I relaxed my body I made up my mind to want to trot. This time under my gentle urging, Truly lowered her head and her pace evened out into a sustained trot.

Wow - success! After 20 minutes of practice, Truly and I both re-learned how to trot. Relaxation and want- to were vital ingredients.

Riding with relaxation at a trot was great, but it took effort and concentration. Shouldn't relaxing be easy and, "relaxed?" Much has been written on horse-whispering and helping horses overcome fear. Why couldn't I find something written specifically on overcoming human fear?

My shelf full of horse books described how to ride well, but there seemed to be a gap, a huge missing puzzle piece when it came to confidence.

Back in my Army-wife days, I had drawn a cartoon of an Army lieutenant mapping out a flow chart on a chalkboard. In the cartoon the lieutenant's superior officer carefully read the complicated progression of information in a problem solving exercise. Then pointing to the small section bearing the words, "AND THEN A MIRACLE HAPPENS," the officer commented, "Nice work lieutenant, but I'd like a little more detail in this area."

This cartoon portrayed exactly how I felt. Though I was experiencing progress by putting into practice what I'd read in how-to horse books, nothing described HOW to overcome fear. The assumption seemed to be that if you get on the horse properly and put your body into the right positions while on the horse, you are riding and if you are riding, you must have confidence.

Riding in the arena did increase my confidence level, but the thought of riding down the road was still terrifying. My safe-zone perimeter would have to be stretched to encompass outside the arena. I wondered if forcing myself to ride the road little bits at a time would help me find the miracle that I needed to happen.

I began sneaking little road rides when nobody was around to watch me. My fear was an embarrassing problem that I tried to keep hidden.

First I rode down the driveway to the mailbox and back. Then I went a few tenths of a mile towards the intersection. I rode back and forth until I felt a little better about being outside the arena. The potential of having a runaway was always on my mind, but at least I had made it outside the arena on a horse. It was time for a test ride with a trusted friend on a calm horse - someone who would humor my odd request to ride with me, no matter what.

Chapter 10 – A Ride to Decide

"Don't let me bail out." I shouted to Gary who was riding ahead of me on his big black mule. Many hours of practice riding Truly in the arena did help me feel better about riding but I was a long way from being comfortable.

My mouth was dry. I had a death grip on the saddle horn and while I was not clamping the saddle with my legs, I sat hunched over in a fetal-position. The test ride had started out quietly, but as we approached an intersection on the gravel road, Truly stiffened and raised her head towards the sound of hammers where a new home was being built.

"Here it comes" I thought. "She's going to freak." Sure enough, Truly began dancing sideways and snorting. "Oh God, what am I doing on this horse?"

With shaking hands I pulled the left rein and circled Truly to slow her dancing. That gravel road intersection became a decision point for me. Would I continue trying to ride or would I dismount and walk away from riding horses forever?

Gary stopped at the intersection and waited for me to ride Truly up beside him. The look on his face made it clear that he could not figure out why I was having so much trouble riding a 15-year-old kid-broke quarter pony that I had trained myself and ridden for years.

"I really want to be able to ride with you, Donna." Gary said, his voice full of frustration.

"Ok." I replied, "I'll keep trying if you will help me. Humor me, ride with me slowly. Make me ride up and down this road with you, and - don't take anything personally." I managed a halfhearted smile.

We turned right on the gravel road and continued riding. Truly was as stiff as a springboard ready for the worst. Terrified, tears ran down my cheeks as I squeezed my eyes shut and tried to regain control.

I coached myself, "Relax and breathe in - 2-3-4-

…relax and breathe out –2-3-4- out...in 2-3-4…out 2-3-4"

Thanks to Gary's bewildered persistence we rode back and forth up and down the road until I felt comfortable enough to venture down a trail alongside a neighbor's hayfield.

I didn't enjoy the hayfield ride, but it awakened memories of the days when I lived for the love of riding. As we headed for the barn, I silently decided to keep trying to get back into the saddle. The missing ingredient to overcoming fear seemed to involve understanding how fear had changed my mental focus. I would have to place myself under a microscope and study the origin and evolution of my fear. I began in earnest.

I thought back to my entry into the world of horse - learning to ride on the military rental horses who had many tricks for getting the upper hoof over their riders. At age 36, I was well into the self preservation stage of life. Because I had enjoyed a long stretch of beginner's luck I remember wondering how it would feel to fall off a horse.

That question had been answered when I was riding Texas Red with my bareback bronc rig instead of a saddle. We had taken a short cut off the trail to get to the road and stirred up a nest of yellow jackets. Texas Red began bucking to fling the stinging creatures off his legs. I grabbed for the bronc rig but missed the little leather handle. Instead of struggling to remain on Texas red's back, I resigned myself to the fact that I was going to be bucked off. I hit the ground, rolled over my shoulder and using momentum stood back upright.

"That was easy!" I exclaimed in disbelief.

After Texas Red settled down, I led him to a tree stump and pulled myself back up onto his withers. I'd read that it was important to get back on a horse immediately after a fall. Instead of fear, I felt a surge of confidence.

My second unplanned exit from a horse's back was as I was leading a trail ride through the woods. I had been looking back and talking to riders behind me when a squirrel scampered across the trail underneath Texas Red's hind feet.

Texas Red took off like a shot leaving me lying on my back looking up at the trees with my right hand underneath me. I jammed and twisted a finger which sustained a compound fracture.

After a trip to the emergency room, I returned to the riding stable and continued leading guided trail rides with a cast from my finger to my elbow. Fear was not a factor. Mounting with one hand was the only difficult result of my unplanned butt-first dismount.

Over the years I've had a number of unexpected exits from the saddle with no lasting negative effects. Falling off a horse did not seem to be the cause of my fear.

The first time I remembered feeling raw fear was during a runaway.

One evening after work, we trail guides decided to ride down the gravel road to the river and relax. I was mounted on gentle bombproof "Skeeter."

We started off at a trot and then moved into an easy

lope down a straight stretch of the road. Exhilarated by the increased pace, someone yelled, "Let's run!" The stable manager who was riding with us, responded with hesitation, "I don't know 'bout that - we may git somebody hurt."

Throwing his words of caution to the wind, we kicked our horses up into a gallop. Initially it was thrilling! Skeeter's long mane whipped my face, blinding me.

I tried repositioning my hands on the reins for a firmer grip, but instead of leather I ended up with fistfuls of long flowing mane. The reins were tangled in Skeeter's mane and I was losing control.

"Ok, I've had enough!" I yelled into the wind. "Let's STOP!"

Nobody stopped. Our horses continued racing down the road. All I could do was hang on and pray that Skeeter would eventually run out of energy.

The horses finally tired and slowed, enabling us to find the whoa-gear. I dismounted, panting as hard as Skeeter, turned to the stable manager angrily, "Didn't you hear me yelling to stop?"

He pointed to his puffing horse and said, "I wuz a tryin' to stop. Look at the saddle a way up on his neck. I wuz a pullin' back hard. I couldn't circle him a'cause I was a'feared he'd fall plum over and we'd all end up in a wreck."

That incident remained deeply ingrained in my subconscious. When fear of riding began creeping up on me, falling off wasn't the problem - I was terrified of having another runaway. I feared losing control.

My riding confidence began to fade after Amy's untimely death. Initially I was not aware that I was losing confidence. I incorrectly assumed that my horse, Ellie, was developing a mysterious fear of goats.

When I'd ride Ellie down the road I deeply missed my daughter Amy, my riding buddy. Grief, anger and loss were powerful emotions that I kept to myself, but my horse knew something was wrong. The turmoil of anguish was reflected in my body, and transferred to my horse. She felt my tension, helplessness and rage.

Ellie's sudden display of a fear of goats made no sense at the time. We had ridden down the road past the neighbor's goat herd hundreds of times before and Ellie never paid attention to them. Out of the blue Ellie began snorting, sidestepping, and whirling to run back to the barn whenever she saw the goats. My steadfast mare was becoming unpredictable and easily spooked.

As I analyzed and pieced together the past, I began to gain insight into bombproof Ellie's sudden apparent fear of goats. On the surface I dealt well with Amy's death but my hidden emotions were painful and tumultuous. Ellie tuned in to me as I rode, and responding to what she sensed. "As I thought in my heart, so was my horse."

When I lost Ellie to founder and began working with two-year-old Truly, I felt increasing insecurity. Mounting a young horse for the first time understandably involves uncertainty, but lurking in the recesses of my mind was the growing fear of losing control.

Truly responded beautifully to training despite my

inner qualms and became a trustworthy mount. During her 15 years of wearing a saddle, Truly earned the title "bombproof horse" many times over.

A novice adult rider was mounted on Truly in a group ride down the road. Truly began trotting to keep up with the longer legged horses. After bouncing in the saddle for several steps, the novice rider said to Truly, "Oh no! Please WALK!" Immediately Truly slowed down. The amazed rider said, "Wow! This horse is voice activated!"

I felt confident putting anyone on Truly's back - anyone except myself. Realizing the nature of my fear gave me hope. I was determined to find the missing ingredient to the miracle of me once again riding without fear.

Runaway!

Part III – Becoming Bombproof

Truly is a bombproof horse.
I needed to become a bombproof rider
to get back in her saddle and put a smile on her face.

Chapter 11 - Find Power in Smiling

Truly is an "easy keeper." To keep her weight down and prevent foundering, Truly must be moved for several hours each day out of the big corral where the horses have free access to a round bale of hay. In the summer Truly spends summer nights in the riding arena with a bedtime snack flake of hay.

One evening instead of leading Truly to the riding arena for her overnight stay away from the round bale of hay, I impulsively tried riding her bareback to her evening quarters.

I tied the loose end of Truly's lead rope onto the bottom ring of her halter creating a looped rein and led her to an overturned tub. She stood still as I awkwardly threw a leg over her back and settled into position just behind her withers.

I felt every muscle in Truly's back move when she merely shifted her weight.

"What am I doing on a horse without a saddle?!"

"I better get off."

"That's great, Donna! I've always said that riding bareback is the best way to learn balance." Gary said as he appeared around the corner of the barn.

Gary's encouragement over-rode my thoughts of bailing out. I didn't want to disappoint him or look like a total chicken.

Carefully I eased Truly across the barnyard and towards the riding arena clutching a fistful of mane and holding desperately onto her belly with my legs. The unfamiliar feel of muscle and bone moving beneath me made me feel very insecure, but we made it to the arena.

Surprisingly, the arthritis in my hip felt better from the brief close contact with Truly's warm back. I began doing some self-physical therapy and worked on being even more "with" Truly by riding bareback a little bit every day.

Pat Parelli's instruction, "Smile with all your cheeks" from in his book *Natural Horsemanship* came to mind each time I climbed up on Truly's back for my daily bareback ride.

"I wonder how you smile with your butt." I chuckled as I settled into place and directed Truly towards the riding arena with a smile on my face, wondering if my butt was following suit.

My two-minute bareback ride to the arena was becoming a familiar event. Truly walked on her own to my makeshift mounting block and waited for me to climb on her back and ride to the flake of hay awaiting her.

I was learning the feel of moving closely with the horse. It was a huge difference from sitting on top of a saddle and using my feet in stirrups keep my balance. Breathing in and out in sync with Truly's steps helped me relax and kept my attention from wandering to things that might scare Truly.

One day I stumbled across an article about smiling. Scientists had been studying the muscles in the face, charting which muscles were involved in making various expressions. They discovered that when they tightened the muscles to produce angry faces, they began to feel angry. When making smiling faces, their moods improved and they felt happy.

The concept that our faces are hardwired to our emotions fascinated me. Could putting a smile on my face bring about positive emotions? Fear is a negative emotion. Could smiling be a way to override fear?

Pioneer psychologist William James over 100 years ago researched the question "which comes first the stimulus or the emotion?" James concluded, "Action seems to follow feeling, but really action and feeling go together; and by regulating the action, which is under the more direct control of the will, we can indirectly regulate the feeling, which is not."

Because our facial expressions are so closely connected to our emotions, smiling and looking around you cheerfully will soon make you feel cheerful. Smiling overrides negative emotions.

If your face is tense, your body will be tense. Watch someone struggling to lift a heavy object. As they call upon their muscles for more power, their facial muscles become involved. Research has proven that grimacing increases hand and arm strength.

"Ya didn't hold your tongue right" is a joking reason for a botched project. Many people purse their lips or hold their tongues in a particular way while concentrating on a task involving fine motor skills and coordination.

Psychologist Ben Twerski wrote, "When we create a synthetic smile, we usually experience feelings that flicker between really feeling-good and I'm just faking this and I feel silly."

When you smile you become filled with feelings that match your facial expression. Smile-therapy is used to help depressed patients. People are instructed to "pump smile iron" by activating their zygomaticus (smile muscles) at least three times a day doing sets of six facial muscle tightenings. The positive results are usually immediate.

Before trying the smile theory while riding Truly, I decided to test it while driving. My truck has no response to my emotions, so an over-the-road test would be an evaluation of how smiling would affect me alone.

Winding narrow paved roads scare me. I dislike judging distance while driving around curves. Meeting traffic while negotiating curves on such roads increases my nervousness. I feel myself tense up and squeeze the steering wheel tightly. Gripping the steering wheel tighter actually diminishes ability to control the vehicle. Tight grip contributes to over-steering and fighting with the steering wheel to keep the vehicle on the road.

These facts I knew in my head, but I always felt the instinct to clamp a death grip on the steering wheel when meeting traffic on windy narrow roads. Would smiling help me relax my hands?

"Here comes a big truck. I hate these narrow roads"

I sucked in a deep breath of air and smiled broadly as the eighteen-wheeler approached. Breathing slowly and evenly I continued smiling. I kept my hands firm but sensitive. I could feel my truck's tires steady on the road through the steering wheel. I wasn't afraid. I felt alert and in full control of the vehicle. I smiled the rest of the way home and arrived in a wonderful mood.

When evening feeding time finally I hurriedly fed the goats and grabbed Truly's halter off the peg in the barn.

"Ok Truly, we're trying something new." I said as I pulled my face muscles into an upward curve of a smile.

"There is amazing power in a smile. You, my lady, are going to help me regain confidence and as a bonus, I hope to put a smile on your face as well."

Truly

Chapter 12 - Take Hold of the Reins

Smiling was a surprising piece to the puzzle fell into place. Arena riding was becoming enjoyable. Occasionally Truly would raise her head and alert to something and I would feel the familiar rush of fear, but a smile and renewed concentration on breathing in sync with her footsteps squelched rising panic.

Smiling and breathing control which worked beautifully in the comfort zone of the arena still failed me when the road. There were too many distractions and potential scary things out there. Something was still missing in solving the rest of the fear puzzle.

"Ok, Truly, I'm not ready for the road yet. All I know to do is keep practicing riding you bareback. I'll learn to sit to your trot better and I'll refine my communication skills. You can work on responding to my cues. Deal?"

Truly nuzzled my pocket for another piece of apple and I suddenly realized I was hiding behind treats. My motive for giving Truly treats was not simply because she enjoys snacks, but to bribe her into being "good".

"I'm always so worried that you won't like me, girl." I confided as Truly pushed my hand with her nose, demanding another treat.

"Because I don't want to upset you I have a hard time insisting that you do as I ask. I let you invade my space because I don't want you to be mad at me."

My throat tightened and I felt a knot in my stomach as insight washed over me. I was so afraid of upsetting a horse that I let Truly get away with pushing me around. I went out of my way to be nice and make Truly happy by giving her what I thought she wanted, hoping she would be nice to me in return.

The same was true with people. I had been raised to be a good person, to put others before myself, not to be selfish or disagreeable. I withheld my feelings, opinions, wants and needs to avoid upsetting, disappointing, or offending people.

I wasn't being honest and open. I was always trying to win people's favor by not making waves that may rock their boats. People mistook my silence for agreement. As a result my kindness was taken for granted and I was thrust into situations that were good for others but which caused me personal suffering. I felt resentful and out of control of my own life.

"I can't go on like this." I said to Truly and to myself. "I will never again go along with something simply because I am expected to or because I'm afraid of upsetting people."

Blinking tears from my eyes, I scratched Truly's forehead and continued, "If you don't like me, or if people get upset with me - so be it. I've got to take control of my own life."

Before losing Amy, I'd had the distinct feeling that something was wrong with the method of treatment Amy had been receiving for depression, but I was afraid of upsetting the doctors who viewed me as an overbearing mother when I objected to their use of drugs instead of providing counseling for Amy. Against my better judgment I was pressured into allowing the doctors to prescribe the antidepressant for her.

Despite their training, the doctors had been wrong. My inability to follow my intuition and stand up to the doctors, coupled with the horror of finding Amy that morning, left me with an overwhelming feeling of helplessness.

I had been unable to keep Amy safe from the doctors, the antidepressant pills, or her depression. It was the same feeling as being on a runaway horse. I had grabbed for life's reins and had ended up with useless handfuls of mane. I felt powerless.

I stood with my head pressed on Truly's warm neck and allowed the rush of insight to continue.

Riding Ellie had become bittersweet. I loved Ellie and close contact with a horse is healing, but I deeply missed Amy's company. Riding Ellie down the road alone left a gaping hole in the scene where Amy and her pony Lady Blue Eyes had been. Memories flooded me as I rode and I felt the loss of Amy acutely.

Ellie sensed my pain but her horse brain couldn't understand what was causing the turmoil in her rider. All Ellie knew was that something was wrong, so she was on alert for danger.

When the goat herd down the road scuttled about as we approached, Ellie translated the heightened negative emotion she sensed in me to, "Ah, goats. They must be threatening my rider. I'll take us to the safety of the barn."

My human brain evaluated Ellie's sudden fear of goats as unreasonable and I began to worry about what else may cause her to spook.

Eventually pain from losing a loved one eases and healing takes place. I felt better about life and tried to use the negative experience to become a better person. With my feet on the ground, I did become a stronger person, but when I climbed into the saddle my confidence was gradually eroding. I didn't realize that the problem of a spooky horse was being caused by my own inner turmoil.

A few years later, experiencing sexual harassment and retaliation at work made me fear for my personal safety. I hated going to work. Home was my refuge, but after letting the needy family stay at my farm, even home become unpleasant. I began to resent their presence on my property.

Their fighting among themselves and using my belongings without respect for my property took its toll. They ignored my request to honor how I wanted things done in my own home and barnyard. The sheriff frequently was needed to settle their disputes.

Cussing, fussing and bad behavior was their norm, but if I expressed a dislike or emphatically said "no" to something, all hell would break loose. If I expressed irritation or strong dislike for something, they were horrified. I wasn't supposed to get mad – I was the agreeable one!

I hated being at work and I hated going home. I wanted to be kind and do the Christian thing by giving help to people in need but I had no say about my own property. I felt I was just along for the ride - out of control.

After the family had found a place to live, they continued to expect favors. The wanted to borrow my truck, to use my washing machine. They asked for money and rides to town.

They weren't in my yard any more, but I still felt pressured to be nice, do what they wanted and help them when they demanded. What I wanted or what was important to me was never considered. I was expected to be constantly kindhearted and giving.

"I've had enough!" I said as I gently pushed Truly's startled face away from my pocket. "When I lost Amy I said I would always listen to red flags, to my intuition. I need to stand by that promise."

"I will never again go against intuition and furthermore I will never feel obligated to be nice if it means going against what is right for me. I won't violate my conscience just to avoid upsetting other people."

111

"If people don't like me for my following my gut and for not allowing myself to be pushed around and used - well tough! They can choose to stay away from me. If they don't like me for standing up for myself, that's okay. I like me and I'm not playing the manipulate-Donna' game any longer!"

My inner resolve gave me instant peace and sense of taking responsibility for my own life. To my surprise, the people I had been so worried about upsetting, were suddenly more considerate of my feelings. The constant asking for favors diminished. By taking charge of my life I wasn't pushing people away, I was teaching people how to treat me with respect.

Accepting responsibility for directing my own life brought me a sense of being in control. The next time I swung my leg over Truly's back, I didn't worry about upsetting her by expecting her to do as I asked. With a smile, I assumed leadership and Truly responded by placing confidence in me.

Doing things for other people became a joy instead of

a burden when I was the one who initiated the acts of kindness. I was free to give from my heart instead of feeling obligated and used by other people.

A surprising side-effect of taking responsibility for my own life was a diminished fear of heights. When a contractor failed to finish re-roofing the house, Gary and I were left with the task of hurrying to finish the job ourselves before it rained. I was able to climb the ladder onto the roof with confidence and assist Gary as he nailed down shingles.

Arena riding became a joyous experience rather than an exercise. The feeling of quiet control was a significant breakthrough. Another huge piece of the puzzle fell into place.

It would soon be time for another road test.

114

Chapter 13 - Ride in Real Time

I set Truly's hoof on the ground, wiped my hand on my jeans and answered my cell phone.

"Donna," I heard Gary's voice above the roar of a tractor, "Would you bring me a jug of lemonade. This hayfield is going to take longer than I thought."

Gary had driven the tractor and mower down the road to one of the neighboring hayfields that we were contracted to cut and bale.

"Sure thing." I dropped the hoof pick in the brush box and switched the cell phone to my other ear. "I'll run indoors, make some lemonade and be there in a bit."

Truly watched me shove the phone back in my pocket. She was freshly groomed, her hooves cleaned, it would only take a minute to throw a saddle on her back. "Wait here girl. I've got an idea. I'll be back."

A few minutes later Truly and I were headed down the road with the lemonade jug tied to her saddle horn with bale twine. We were on a mission.

A year of arena riding had brought suppleness back to my body. The arthritis in my hip had settled down - I felt limber and stronger. Riding bareback each day was teaching me to feel Truly and move with her. I was learning true balance instead of merely catching my balance with the stirrups and cantle once my balance had been lost.

Sitting in the saddle I felt slightly higher and my right stirrup felt awkward, but I was relaxed and at ease. The crunch of the gravel under Truly's hooves made a rhythmic sound that was easy to breathe in sync with.

Smiling, breathing, relaxing, looking at the road where I want to go instead of at the horse - these simple things made a huge difference. Taking control of my life was a breakthrough confidence factor.

At the intersection where I had a year earlier experienced my fearful meltdown, I smiled and guided Truly to turn left.

The lemonade jug swung in time with Truly's hoof steps. I was actually enjoying the ride. I thought back to that day I rode with Gary. All it had taken was the unusual sound of hammers wafting on the air to alert Truly to possible danger.

The memory of Truly's raised head, pricked ears and flaring nostrils a year ago came to my mind in a mental image.

"I sure hope there's nothing unusual down the road in this direction." I thought to myself.

As if on cue, Truly raised her head slightly and I felt her walk stiffen. She tipped her nose slightly to the left, asking to turn around and head for home.

"No. We are delivering lemonade." I said firmly. "We aren't done riding yet."

My brief "what if" thought brought back memories of the curious cattle that rushed to the fence and a dog that sometimes appeared out of nowhere.

My breathing was becoming shallow and I had stopped smiling. My mind was whirring with memories and possibilities of what we may lurk down the road.

Truly was becoming agitated. She clearly wanted to turn around and go back to her buddy horses. I was going to have to engage in a battle of will. Bummer! What was wrong with this picture!

We rode tensely a while longer. When I recognized the feel of panic welling up in me, I knew I had to do something different.

"Whoa Truly, look at that!" I pretended to be totally interested in a road-kill turtle. "I want to see that turtle up close."

Instinctively, I felt that it would be counterproductive to let Truly think that fussing would get me off her back. I had to let Truly think I had a different reason for climbing out of the saddle.

I stopped Truly, dismounted and led her to the squashed turtle that had been in the hot sun for a couple days. The smell wafting up from the decaying turtle was noxious.

Using the toe of my boot I slid the odoriferous mass of crushed shell off the road into the ditch. "Okay Truly, let's check your hooves for stones."

Grooming has always had a calming effect on Truly. I dropped one rein to the ground and while carefully holding the other I said, "You're ground-tied, girl, but I'm holding onto one rein just in case you decide to go home without me."

After picking up her feet and finding no rocks, I pulled Truly's girth strap a notch tighter and remounted.

Moving the turtle, checking Truly's feet and tightening her girth were actions that pulled me out of my "what if" mode of thinking about possible road-boogers and put me firmly into the present moment.

"Ok Truly, I'm focused again. Let's deliver this lemonade."

When I arrived at the hayfield on horseback, Gary's face broke into a huge grin. He took a drink of the refreshing liquid and said, "Even better than this lemonade was seeing you riding up the road on horseback."

After a rest in the hayfield, Truly was ready for the return trip home. I was in a hurry to get back to finish chores and Truly anticipated greeting her horse buddies. We had the ingredients for an out of control ride back home.

I gathered the reins, swung my leg over Truly's back and turned to wave goodbye to Gary.

Smile…breathe…relax…look at the road ahead, not at the horse…and don't scan the perimeter for boogers. Don't think about what may happen - focus on right now.

I could feel my mind wanting list all the bad things that could happen on the ride home. I had to rein in my wandering mind.

"No more Miss Pushover for me, Truly." I said aloud.

"I am in control of my life and I won't be intimidated by people any more I won't let my own kindness be used to manipulate me into doing things for other people that I really don't want to do."

Truly's ears flicked back and forth as she listened to me talk.

"I took my life's reins back from other people and I'm not just along for the ride any more. I'm directing my own life."

Talking aloud pulled my focus away from the "what ifs" and locked me into the present moment instead of reliving old fears or worrying about what might pop up down the road.

"Truly, this is pretty awesome. When I'm talking to you like this, I am living in real-time instead of being stuck in re-run or worry mode."

Truly blew dust out of her nose and shook her head slightly.

"When I get on your back and start thinking about what could go wrong, that's living in the future and my fearful anticipation sends you warning signals. You feel my body tension and you know I'm holding my breath, so you are sure that something is wrong."

"There's no way you can know that I'm just thinking ahead to a future possibility. My body sends you the message that what I'm imagining is for real."

I patted Truly's neck and kept talking.

"Because you are a good horse, you respond appropriately to me, your rider. Then when you raise your head to see with your eyes what I see in my mind, I pull on your reins and clamp my legs onto your saddle. Sorry girl for all the times I've confused you with 'go' and 'whoa' at the same time."

Focusing on my voice was keeping my mind from doing the very thing I was talking about - worrying about what could happen. Talking aloud kept my mind busy with the present moment instead of running off anticipating future trouble.

"Truly, the human mind is a wonderful tool for us people to use. It is said that we only use a small percentage of our mind. I think that's because our minds are usually full of whirring thoughts - reviews of past conversations, agonizing over past events, fretting about the future….I think we humans routinely experience full-blown runaway minds."

"You horses don't let your minds run off like that. You will react to a stimulus, but you don't conjure up the stimulus. Food for example - I'd have to shake a can of grain or bite into an apple to present the sight or sound that would make you think of food."

"Runaway minds sap people's energy, cause absent-mindedness and forgetfulness and mistakes. We become stressed by our body's reactions to things in our minds that are long since over or that haven't even happened!"

"Imagination is a wonderful thing and the mind is a wonderful tool. We humans need to use and direct our minds, not let our minds run away with us."

I smiled and took a deep breath. We were a little over halfway home and talking to Truly was indeed keeping my mind from running off to the "what ifs" down the road. I continued,

"People use food, alcohol, sex, TV, games, gambling

- anything that provides a pleasurable focus on the present to rein in thought. Some jobs keep people in the present moment because of required focus and concentration. Jobs that require attention to detail, creativity or lifesaving skills keep people in the present moment. Jobs requiring only repetitive motions allow minds to wander and run away."

"Emergency personnel respond to disasters with a focus on the crisis at hand. Prepared by their training, they have presence- of- mind during emergencies. They don't worry about their actions or if they are good enough; their training clicks in and they do what needs to be done."

"Riding leisurely down the road like we are doing now, without a task to accomplish leaves room for my mind to worry about what may scare you. Riding with a task, like herding cattle, or hurrying to rescue a fallen rider on a trail ride or delivering lemonade to the hayfield puts me in the present moment."

Back at the barn I unsaddled Truly and squeeged the wet saddle marks off her back with a sweat scraper. I felt exhilarated by my successful road ride. Two Bible verses came to mind: "Take no thought for tomorrow" and "Forgetting that which is behind I press on."

"It's interesting Truly, even the Bible recommends living in real time - the present moment." I gave her an apple and led her to the corral where her equine buddies and a round bale of hay waited.

Riding in real time - what a powerful weapon against fear!

Chapter 14 – Ride Your Own Horse

"Truly, I figured out something very important about being happy!"

Fumbling with the buckle on Truly's halter, I continued.

"Even when I direct my own life and stop letting people jerk my chain or use my kindhearted nature against me, there are situations that remain beyond my control. Look at my hands, girl. They are ugly and painful. Simple things like putting a halter on you is a challenge."

I looped the lead rope over Truly's neck and tied the loose end through a halter ring under her chin, turning the rope into a thick, soft rein. Then I stepped onto the second rung of a corral panel, threw my right leg over Truly's back and slid into place behind her withers.

Truly's warm body felt good. I smiled and guided Truly towards the freshly mown and baled hayfield. Riding bareback each day helped me stay limber and kept Truly tuned, toned and willing.

I readjusted my fingers on the lead rope. My hands had become a source of concern and embarrassment to me. A few years before, it had become difficult to open jars and attach pneumatic tools to the end of the air hose. Buttoning my shirt required extreme patience and concentration. I was slowly losing grip strength and fine motor control of my fingers.

Pushing the dust mop and buffing the floors at work had become painful. Even handling spray bottles and opening doors had to be done with great care to avoid pain.

A visit to an arthritis specialist who reviewed blood samples, x-rays, and my medical history confirmed that I have osteoarthritis, wear-and-tear arthritis. The doctor looked at my gnarled hands and told me gently that I would never be able to do a hand commercial - unless it was a commercial for arthritis.

Other than Motrin or Tylenol for pain, no medication

helps osteoarthritis, but the upside is that this form of arthritis doesn't attack the body's organs.

After eight finger surgeries involving joint fusions and surgical removal of spurs and arthritic tissue in my joints, no more repairs could be done. Exercising my fingers constantly to retain their limited flexibility and strength is the only remedy.

I held my hands on Truly's warm neck as we made our way across the hayfield in the crisp morning air. The rising sun illuminated the steam that puffed from Truly's nostrils when she exhaled. I was glad for the protection from the cold air provided by Truly's thick mane.

After years of bumping my fingers and gripping things on my job, I'd just about worn out my finger joints. I didn't realize what was happening at first. I ignored the fact that my knuckles were getting bigger and my fingers were becoming stiff. Gradual joint changes are hard to notice and even harder to accept. I didn't want to even think the word "arthritis". I didn't believe I was old enough to have arthritis.

Painful slow-moving fingers are targets for injury. If I bump into something, it seems as though it will be with a body part that already hurts.

I have to be careful to keep my fingers from getting caught in the rings and buckles on halters and bridles. If my fingertip is in the wrong place at the right time when a horse moves its head, "ouch" doesn't describe the pain I feel.

I can't play the guitar any more or knock on doors. Little things I used to take for granted gradually became difficult. Pain makes it easy to become despondent and hopeless. It is tempting to feel that life is not being fair to me. Bitterness and anger, often companions to pain and disability, eat away at the human soul.

No matter how much I smile, if I climb on Truly's back while feeling upset about my situation or people in my life, things beyond my control, she detects my upset energy and senses that something is wrong.

Even when I am not letting people push my buttons, I still feel out-of-control if I am upset about things I cannot or should not try to change.

One of the great people in the Bible, said, "I've learned whatever state (condition) I am in, to be content." In another place the same person admonished, "Having done all, stand." It's not that we are supposed to just lie around and let life run over us, we are to do what we can, then stand up and be happy with what IS.

I have the responsibility to exercise my hands to keep them functioning. When I've done what I can, it is time to accept the situation and be content.

My hands are not perfect, but they are mine. I have the power to choose to be happy with what I have. That which is beyond my control to change is very much within my power to accept.

We had reached the far corner of the hayfield. I shifted my weight from the inside of my thighs and sat back on my butt. Truly stopped walking on cue and waited. I patted her shoulder and looked up at the sky. Rays from the rising sun were spiking through the orange-rimmed clouds. I filled my lungs deeply with the fresh frosty air.

"Let's go back, girl. I've got to get to work."

Truly perked her ears forward as we headed back to the corral where her breakfast hay awaited. She was obviously happy to be heading back, but remained calm and collected. If I had been discontented with my lot in life or anything, Truly very likely would have reflected my impatient emotions with prancing and head-tossing.

Manipulating situations and other people is born out of fear and discontent. Controlling myself is doable. Controlling other people or situations, even with the most noble of motives, is like reaching over and grabbing the reins of another rider's horse – it holds potential for two horse wrecks. Acceptance of what I cannot or should not control is a position of peace and personal power.

I rode in silence, enjoying the sounds of the world waking up around me. A rabbit bounded out in front of us and froze in fear. Truly's head shot up and I quickly grabbed a handful of her mane for extra stability.

Smiling and synchronizing my breathing to match Truly's hoof steps, I spoke to the rabbit in a soothing voice, "Hey there, we won't hurt you. What a pretty soft coat you have."

Slowing my breathing helped me dispel my startle reaction. Directing my attention toward the rabbit in a cheerful appreciative way kept me in "real time." My mind couldn't drag an old scary scene into the present nor could I fast forward to thinking, "Holy doo-doo...what if Truly spooks?"

Truly dipped her head slightly and watched the rabbit shake its whiskers before whirling into a high speed retreat back to the underbrush.

I let go of Truly's mane and patted her neck.

Accepting the situation and appreciating the rabbit made it easier for me to respond calmly instead of reacting in panic.

"There are so many components to how I deal with fear, Truly. It's like reading a list in my head: Posture, smile, breathe, be in real-time, acceptance - I feel like I'm rummaging through a tool box!"

Back at the barn I slid off Truly and removed her halter. As I shut the corral gate I wondered how I could combine my ride-with-confidence tools into one super-tool that would integrate everything I was learning and make it all instantly available at any time as an ever-present part of my life.

Chapter 15 - Ride With a Quiet Mind

We were in a farm supply store looking for water tank heaters when a book titled, *Horse Follow Closely,* caught my attention. The warm colors of the cover photo showed an American Indian and a horse touching foreheads. Thumbing quickly through the pages, I admired photos of GaWaNi Pony Boy riding bareback with confidence through hilly wooded landscape.

"Here's an interesting book, Gary. The photos show how to ride bareback."

Gary took the book from me and turned the pages with interest. "This is good." he said as he handed it back to me.

I tucked the book under my arm. "I've never had bareback lessons. I'll study this book and you can tell me if I look like I'm sitting in the right place on Truly's back."

Later that week a package arrived from my mom. Tearing aside the wrapping, I uncovered a book titled, *Woman Between the Wind.* In a note inside the book mom said that she thought I would enjoy the book because there was a horse in the story, a wild mustang gentled by an Indian woman.

Side by side the books were strikingly similar in color tones and type fonts. Both covers featured an American Indian. I had the odd feeling that I held in my hands answers to questions I didn't yet know how to ask.

My shelves are lined with books from my mom. She has an uncanny way of sending me just the right book at just the right time.

Since I had already begun reading *Horse Follow Closely,* I decided to continue with GaWiNi Pony Boy's book. I was enjoying learning about my leadership role as a human.

Horses are not people with fur and hooves, they are horses, and as such they operate from the herd point of view. Even in a herd of two, a horse and a rider, there must be a leader. When a human climbs onto a horse's back giving off signals of uncertainty or fear, the horse must assume leadership.

During my "decision point ride" down the road with Gary, my fear transferred the responsibility of leadership to Truly who in turn looked to Gary's mount for direction. My feeling that Gary was riding both his horse and Truly was pretty accurate. This explained why group riding is easier for insecure people, as long as the lead rider remains under control.

Along with learning to be a better leader, I began learning to ride bareback with more finesse. To mount I still needed a block, tree stump, or fence rail. My 57-year-old muscles and joints didn't have the spring to jump up on a horse from the ground. Falling off was a different matter. Gravity makes falling off a horse pretty easy – landing is the hard part.

"Today I'm going to practice falling off Truly."

137

Gary looked at me as though I had just arrived from another planet.

"Think about it, Gary. You army soldiers learned how to fall properly so you wouldn't get hurt when landing a parachute or jumping off obstacles, so if I have a plan that I know how to execute in case I do start falling or need to bail off Truly, I'll be less likely to get hurt."

Falling off Truly, first from a standstill and then from a walk, took my confidence level up a notch. I practiced tuck-and-roll procedures to distribute weight evenly and avoid bruising a single landing point on my body. It was almost fun, though Gary said that Truly had a worried look from losing her rider so many times.

With "falling safely" added to my bag of riding-with-confidence tools it was becoming harder to keep my tools from becoming jumbled. Smiling, breathing, staying in the present moment, personal leadership, acceptance of what is - I felt as though I were running a pre-flight checklist whenever I mounted a horse. I wanted these tools to become a natural part of me.

As I began Reading *Woman Between the Wind* I was drawn into the narrative describing a life-changing encounter between a Native American woman and the author. Learning to live with a quiet mind through the relaxed focus of soft vision brought the author to a place of strength and peace.

"Soft vision" was a new phrase to me, but as I explored how it works, I was startled to realize it was something I had done even as a child. When I was in grade school I discovered I could diffuse my vision as though I were looking through a wide-angle lens. I'd relax and slightly cross my eyes to where I could see a wide view. By not focusing on anything in particular, I could see everything. Then I'd tighten my eyes and stare at an object until peripheral vision faded and all I could see was the object I was intently focused upon.

Going back and forth between that soft wide-angle view and a hard focused view was entertaining when I was bored while listening in school. Soft vision was something I had played with not realizing its value.

Intrigued, I searched libraries and the internet for more information on Soft vision.

I read about many ways to enter soft vision. The clearest description I found was:

Look straight ahead at the most distant object in your field of vision. Now cross your eyes slightly, so that your field of vision is blurred and seen in double vision. Spread your awareness evenly in an ever larger circle until you are aware of the entire field of vision. Soften your eyes with a smile (smiling with your eyes, not grinning with your mouth!). Completely relax the eyes without any attempt to influence what or how they see. Rather than focusing on a specific object and jumping from object to object, the eyes become equally aware of your entire field of vision, and they rest softly without jumping around. As the eyes relax, so the mind becomes calm. Smile with your eyes and allow that smile to soften your face and spread throughout your body. Focusing on nothing, you become aware of everything.

Soft vision quiets the mind and diffuses negative emotions. When eyes and face are relaxed and nothing in particular is being stared at, anger and fear dissolve. Racing thoughts slow down. Instead of being bombarded by thoughts, fragments of conversations, when we operate in soft vision we are in control of our minds and our feelings.

Staring intently is useful when we need to decipher or understand something. When we are focusing on a problem or situation, our eyes narrow, our mouths tighten, our muscles contract and our peripheral vision fades. Our bodies are tense and ready for action and our thoughts run with possibilities, questions and answers.

Often, when we are done problem-solving, we do not leave the position of hard focus. It is like leaving the computer on, up and running even when not in use. As a result, our minds race with nonstop thoughts.

When sitting on the back of a horse initially trying to battle fear, the focus of my attention had been on fear itself as I struggled to understand and overcome the debilitating emotion. My concentrated focus on fear accelerated my whirring thoughts and physical tension.

When I discovered the value of keeping my mind in the present moment I was able to deal with what was actually happening instead of fearing what may happen. My mind was quiet instead of dredging up past or future negativity.

As I experimented, I realized that soft vision kept me living in the present moment easily, as a natural way of being. I didn't have to struggle to find the right confidence tool. Living in soft vision predominantly throughout the day gave me a new inner calm.

Negative imagery of losing my daughter and sexual harassment on the job were burned into my memory. Anger and fear, natural responses to being victimized, had been wrapped around me like a protective cloak. I lived with a generalized fear of losing control of my safety and wellbeing. Living tensely tales a huge toll on muscles, joints, teeth, eyes and nerves.

Learning to ride in "real time" instead of thinking back or projecting forward was a breakthrough in overcoming fear, but it required my conscious effort to control my breathing, smile, and maintain a focus on the present moment.

To my surprise, by simply relaxing my eyes and entering soft vision, I didn't need to consciously conjure up my riding-with-confidence tools – they were there, a part of my life experience. Soft vision brought confidence tools into effect without my having to run through the mental checklist. All I had to do was take a deep breath, smile with my eyes, while gently loving all I see.

The puzzling statement, "love casts out fear." suddenly made sense. Instead struggling to conjure up a magic feeling of love, my quiet mind and gentle appreciation of all that I saw produced in me peace and confidence.

☺

"What a way to start the day!." I breathed in the fresh morning air as I enjoyed a quick ride on Truly before heading to work.

"A few years ago, Truly, I would have never believed that I would ever be riding you bareback across a hayfield. You, my friend, have been through a lot with me, and I appreciate your help."

The frosty hayfield sparkled as the rising sun's rays bathed the scene in a rosy glow. Truly's feet crunched on the stiff grass. Steam blew from her nostrils.

The wide panoramic view I saw with relaxed vision was beautiful. I felt totally at ease and happy. I rested my hands on Truly's withers, feeling her warm body soothe my fingers.

"I'm glad I didn't bail out and turn you into a pasture pretty. It's been a hard road, but you helped me understand that I didn't need a bombproof horse - you needed me to become a bombproof rider!"

Truly wiggled her ears back and forth as she listened to me talk.

"I am so glad I found a way to move from paralyzing fear into confidence, peace and personal power."

Chapter 16 – Clear the Grudge Trail

The phone rang while I was preparing supper after evening chores. I handed the spatula to Gary, pointed at the frying pan and hurried answer the phone. The name on caller ID was unfamiliar.

"Hello, This is Donna."

A male voice greeted me, "Hello Ma'am, I'm with the Legion Riders, and Ma'am," He took a deep breath, "I don't want to upset you, but I wanted to call you regarding your daughter."

A glance at the area code on caller ID indicated the call came from the town where Amy had died. A flash of memory made me wince. While the town itself held many wonderful memories of Amy, I hated that place.

"Ma'am," I heard the male voice say, "I know your daughter died in 1993, and…"

My mind leaped ahead of the voice. He must be calling about the wrongful death suit that was settled out of court in 1995, but why's he calling now?

"…we have found her remains and wish to give her a proper burial on Memorial Day along with forgotten soldiers who we will be honoring. This will be at no cost whatsoever to you, Ma'am."

I swallowed hard and walked to the kitchen, my attention riveted on the stranger's voice.

"We came across your name, and we always try to notify any next of kin that we find. We just need to verify your daughter's father's social security number and…"

Was this some kind of horrible telemarketing scheme? How could he be talking about finding Amy? After her autopsy she was cremated and then, while I never knew what had been done with her ashes, I assumed people's cremains were properly taken care of automatically - but I never really knew. I had come to hate Memorial Day as I had nowhere to remember Amy. Her beloved horse Truly was her living memorial.

"Donna, what's wrong." The alarm in Gary's voice jolted me back to the phone call.

"Just a minute, you say you have my daughter's remains?" I repeated for Gary to hear, "And you want to provide a burial for her?"

Gary's eyes reflected my own shock and disbelief.

"Yes, Ma'am. I know this must be hard for you. I apologize. I never want to upset people...."

Something in the man's voice rang true. He seemed kind, concerned and genuine.

"Sir, I want to believe you. I really didn't have any idea what became of my daughter's ashes, but if this is true is there any way that I can have her sent here to me? And could I please have a day to think about this, and no offence, but to check this out? May I call you back tomorrow with a decision?

"I understand completely Ma'am." The man sounded relieved.

After writing down the man's call back number, and the number of the funeral home where he claimed to have found Amy's cremains, I numbly set down the phone and looked at Gary. "What do I do.?

"You will check it out tomorrow, and we will take it from there." He replied. "If the call is genuine, we will give your daughter a proper burial."

The next day I learned that the Legion Riders are motorcycle-riding members of The American Legion who work with funeral homes to bury forgotten remains of veterans with military honors.

A call to the funeral home verified that Amy's cremains had indeed been there for 15 years. In the records was a handwritten note from a phone conversation: "The father called and said they will not be picking up their daughter's cremains."

I remembered my x-husband, Amy's father, saying to me, "It is only a body," to which I had agreed, thinking he was trying to make me feel better about Amy death by stating in a nondescript way that her soul lives on. I had no idea he intentionally left Amy's cremains at the funeral home.

By the end of the day arrangements were made for Amy to be sent to me. I worried that the initial paralyzing fear I felt 15 years ago would return.

When Amy's cremains arrived, I drove home with the small but surprisingly heavy package in the passenger seat. It seemed natural to talk.

"Amy I've got a farm now and your horse, Truly, is doing great. You can be proud of her. I planted a rose bush for you. Truly and the roses have been my way of remembering you. I've missed you."

At home, I carefully carried the box containing Amy's cremains to the barn and called Truly. She came running to the gate.

"Truly, you were a baby when you lost your owner - here she is again. We can say goodbye to Amy properly now."

Truly nuzzled the box, ears flicking. I patted her and

smiled.

"I've got to go and call the priest now, and find out what needs to be done to provide a funeral mass and burial."

Everything a funeral home automatically takes care of had to be done ourselves. The first challenge was finding a contact for the local cemetery so I could purchase a plot. Cemetery phone numbers are not listed in the phone book.

Once the burial plot was purchased and I had its real estate title in hand, Gary and I used a tractor and auger to dig the hole. We made a temporary marker, our Priest conducted funeral mass and burial ceremony after which Gary and I closed the grave and replaced the sod ourselves. I designed a headstone patterned after the horse drawing Amy had given me the night before she died.

Gary and I honored Amy's life in providing a funeral mass and burial. Truly no longer carried the burden of being Amy's memorial. The weight of uncertainty was lifted and I felt the peace of closure.

Laying Amy to rest with honor befitting her was a real

action with symbolic significance that propelled me into even deeper healing. I began to lay the pain and hurt of the past to rest.

For many years I had dutifully prayed for my enemies. I prayed that those who harmed me would be brought to a place in life of "their highest good" but It was a struggle to pray. The hurtful deeds of other people still littered my past and caused me pain.

I began to realize that I had the power to forgive those who had acted in hatred or ignorance toward me. I let go of my "right" to be angry at those whose actions had harmed me. Forgiveness does not excuse or condone wrongdoing - hurtful acts will be dealt with by the justice system, God or Karma - it is much simpler for me to treat people with compassion and let them rest in the hands of the powers that be.

Forgiveness, the final piece in my puzzle in becoming a bombproof human, is necessary to live in the place of personal power, in "real time."

I cannot remain in the present moment if I allow my mind to return with self righteous anger to the past. If I hold a grudge, the past is replicated in the present and prolongs my pain as I relive the event over and over.

When a person plants corn, corn is what grows not tomatoes.. This is karma but I call it farm theology. We harvest exactly what we plant. If we plant harm to others, we reap harm. If we plant kindness we harvest kindness. If we plant forgiveness we find peace. By forgiving, I free myself from the pain of the past so I can live in the present moment, without worrying about other people's crops.

☺

"Amy, losing you has been very difficult. I miss you. I've been angry at you for leaving me because it hurt. I could never understand what you felt in your heart, but I know you never intended to cause me pain, and I'm sorry you felt such pain.

I love you, my sweet Amy, and I hope you are proud of your horse, Truly. She has helped me find a way to become a bombproof human. I hope that in becoming bombproof I have put a smile on Truly's face, and Amy, I hope you are smiling too."

Amy riding Rose

Chapter 17 – Bombproof Yourself

You can find confidence in riding and in life. If you think you can or can't – you are probably right.

A successful weight- loss diet is more than enthusiastically counting calories to shed a few pounds only to slide back to old eating habits that cause weight gain.

Developing inner confidence is not something you experiment with for a while and then forget about. Becoming bombproof involves a gradual lifestyle change.

The following exercises are simple but powerful and will bring you to a place of confidence in your life. The exercises are designed specifically for a person who wants to handle and ride horses without fear but becoming a bombproof human enhances all areas of life.

Body Language

Our posture speaks volumes to people and animals

around us, and most importantly to ourselves. Riding with good posture prevents back and neck strain and conveys to the horse that you are a confident rider.

If you go about the day with your shoulders hunched forward, you emit the appearance of uncertainty or victim-hood. Animals read human body language. Approaching or mounting your horse with slouched shoulders transmits a message of uncertainty rather than leadership.

Fatigue and depression are two contributors to poor posture. Sitting at a desk or computer terminal with a C curve in your spine promotes fatigue. Rounded shoulders with arms extended forward places strain on rotator cuffs and is a major cause of shoulder and neck pain.

Even as you are reading this book you may be in a slouched position. Sit up straight, take a deep breath, pull your shoulders back and push out your chest as you try to touch your shoulder blades together. Notice your refreshed positive feeling and the immediate relief of neck and back tension.

When I couldn't afford surgery for severe shoulder pain due to a torn rotator cuff, my orthopedic surgeon instructed me to strengthen my back muscles by pulling my shoulders back and pushing my chest out, doing several repetitions throughout the day. It took a year, but I no longer have any shoulder pain and I don't need surgery. As my posture improved, so did my energy and outlook. I sent a positive message to others and to myself through my body language.

Try it! Sit up straight. Gently squeeze your shoulders back slowly pulling your shoulder blades together, push out your chest and hold the position for a count of five. Do this five times. You will feel a pleasant pull in your tight muscles and tendons.

Moving your shoulders back releases tension in muscles that have been strained from a forward hunch. With your shoulders back you have room to take a nice deep breath, really filling your lungs. Deep breathing provides vital oxygen to brain cells and is refreshing and relaxing.

We live in a "leaning forward" generation. Sitting at the computer, driving, working around the kitchen or office, people tend to reach forward with their arms and shoulders, causing slouching.

Make a conscious effort to practice good posture throughout the day. You will feel positive, more energetic, and you will help your body and mind become ready for the saddle.

Self-Image

With good posture, shoulders back and head level, go for a walk around the block, down the road or simply walk around inside your home or workplace.

As you walk, slowly breathe in for a measured number of steps, then exhale for the same number of steps. Get a rhythm going. The goal is to slowly and deeply fill your lungs, then totally empty them in an evenly controlled manner. Breathe in – 2 – 3 – 4 Out 2 – 3 – 4 and so on.

When it feels natural to breathe in time with your

footsteps, begin to focus on your goals. Think of words that describe what you want to be and repeat the words mentally in sync with your footsteps and breathing.

As you put your whole body into walking and breathing with rhythm you can rebuild your-self image by thinking words that describe you as you wish to be. As we think, so we are. Total mind and body involvement reinforces your desired new image.

For example: "I am confident, competent, kind, calm, beautiful, balanced, graceful, strong."

As you walk, make it a game to think of words and break them into syllables that follow the rhythm of your footsteps. Shoulders back, head erect, walk with a firm step and fluid motion, and fill your mind with words that describe the qualities you want to attain. Think positively, as though these qualities already exist in your life. As you think, so you are.

Renovating your self-image lays important groundwork for feeling positive and confident when you swing your leg over the horse's back to ride.

Smile

Our faces are hardwired to our emotions. If you put your face into a scowl, you will feel negative and depressed. When you put smile on your face, you will begin to feel your mood lighten.

Stand in front of the bathroom mirror and watch as you pull your mouth into a smile. Feel the muscles in your cheeks contract. These are your zygomatic muscles, your smile muscles.

You have the ability to smile with your mouth and not involve your eyes. Make a fake smile and watch your eyes. They aren't smiling. Sometimes people put a fake smile on their faces but retain anger or negative emotions which are transmitted by squinty tense eyes.

Look in the mirror and smile with your mouth, relax your eyes and let the smile shine right up through your eyes. A genuine smile brings a twinkle to your eyes. This is the smile that improves your mood. Smiling dispels negative emotions, including the negative emotion of fear. Practice exercising your smile, in front of a mirror and wherever you are throughout the day until smiling becomes a habit.

Horses' facial expressions often reflect the expression of their rider. Next time you pick up a horse magazine, take a moment to thumb through quickly and look at the pictures of horses being ridden. If the rider is smiling or has relaxed facial muscles, the horse generally has a relaxed interested expression as well. If the rider is grimacing or looks tense or angry, the horse's face often carries similar expressions.

Flexibility

A warm up session is recommended before participating in sports or exercise. Flexibility prevents damage to muscles, tendons, and ligaments. Stretching muscles and tendons before riding is a great way to limber up and to enhance your balance. Before climbing into the saddle, gently stretch your riding muscles.

Holding onto the back of a chair, relax and breathe in and out deeply and regularly as when walking. Move your legs slowly one at a time – to the side, forward, backward, and feel for any tension or tightness. To improve your balance, try letting go of the back of the chair as you lift your leg in all directions.

When you notice a tight place, gently extend that muscle or tendon until you feel a slight pull, hold for a count of 5 and relax. Never bounce while stretching. Muscles have memory which is activated by the force of bouncing. Muscles shorten and tighten when bouncing in order to protect themselves. Stretch gently.

Be creative - search out tense or stiff areas in your body. Rotate your ankles, alternately flex and straighten your fingers, rotate your wrists, move your arms in all directions, slowly rotate your head and neck.

As you gently stretch physically, move towards inner flexibility as well. Let your mind accept what you cannot change. If it is cold outside or hot, accept the weather as being okay. If someone near to you has a belief, habit, or quirk that irritates you, stop trying to change that person. Instead change your attitude and accept what you cannot change.

As you breathe in and out to let go of tension, manipulation, worry and wishing things were different - let go of everything you cannot or should not control. We each must ride our own horse, literally and figuratively. Reaching over to grab the reins from another rider's hands will hinder your ability to ride your own horse. So it is in life! Attempting to change other people or situations will complicate your life and make you feel out of control.

Smile, breathe and expand your muscles...experience inner acceptance and peace. Focus on the present moment and feel your body becoming flexible. Flexibility is strength. Feel the strength of inner flexibility as you gain physical flexibility.

Inner flexibility is vital to a having a calm relaxed

attitude which your horse will feel and respond to as your flexible muscles enable you to move with your horse in the saddle.

Humming

Talking to your horse keeps your mind focused on the present moment instead of worrying about bad things that could happen or remembering and dragging past fears into the picture. Humming a tune is just as effective as talking.

The exercise of humming a single note in meditation I've found very helpful to calm my mind.

Take a deep breath, keeping your eyes open listening to the sounds around you. Relax your face muscles by smiling softly with your mouth and your eyes, gently loving all you see. Breathe in slowly and deeply, then exhale slowly while humming a single note. Keep humming the note until your lungs are empty, then slowly re-fill your lungs and resume humming. Do this for five to ten minutes.

You can hum a high note or a low note, whatever fits

the moment or whatever may match a sound you hear in the environment. When you are driving you can practice this method of quieting your mind by humming in tune with the sound of the tires on the road or the vehicle's engine sound.

This humming exercise improves your lung capacity and health as well as calming your nerves and quieting your mind. Your body will benefit from sufficient oxygen supply. Shallow breathing which accompanies tension and fear, can lower the oxygen count in your blood. Lower oxygen levels can contribute to headaches, aggravate asthma and hinder your body's healing process.

You will notice that humming quiets your racing thoughts. You experience quiet alertness and attention to the present moment. When distracting thoughts try to jump into your mind, simply notice the thoughts and resume humming. You will train yourself to breathe deeply, relax, and keep a quiet mind.

Soft Vision

Soft Vision is a way of "looking" that places you in your seat of personal power. We live in a tense hunched-forward generation. People sit at the computer with shoulders rounded, arms forward, intently staring at the computer screen performing job duties, social networking or playing games.

The state of New York provides online instructions for workers who spend long hours in front of computer terminals. Computer technicians are instructed to sit up, stretch, improve posture and relax their eyes by entering Soft Vision.

Soft Vision is the opposite of staring. When you stare at an object, your eyes tense and your mind races with the activity of deciphering, examining, or calculating. Analytical thinking is necessary in life, but when you are done working on a problem, it is important to relax your mental grip and let your mind rest. Soft Vision quiets the mind.

Try staring at an object in the distance. Notice that while staring you have tunnel vision. Your attention is focused on that one object. This is "Hard Vision. Now smile and let your eyes relax and twinkle with your smile. Slightly cross your eyes and notice that you can see a wider view when you stop staring at a single object.

Experiment with moving back and forth between Hard and Soft Vision. Notice the differences in your field of vision and in how you feel.

Eastern religions practice Soft Vision, sometimes called Soul Vision, by instructing people to be aware of the place in the center of the forehead called the "third eye". Imagining that you are seeing through the center of your forehead can be helpful in achieving Soft Vision.

A simple way to relax your mind and quiet your thoughts with Soft Vision is by smiling. Smiling lifts the mood and dispels negativity because. Smiling is a natural way to enter Soft Vision. To quiet your mind with Soft Vision, smile softly with your eyes, gently loving all you see.

When you smile and let your eyes reflect your smile, it becomes easy to quietly accept everything you see. Negative emotions dissipate. Your mind becomes quiet, and your horse responds by relaxing and trusting your leadership.

The human mind is very much like a computer. It is frustrating when our computer locks up and stops responding to our requests. It is likewise frustrating when our mind runs amuck with fear, anger, worry or boredom.

Soft Vision will help you quiet your thoughts, remain in the present moment, and take control of your emotions. When you are at peace in life you will have a positive effect on the people and animals around you. It is like a vortex of positive energy that spreads to those you care about.

When someone in your presence becomes angry, Soft Vision will help you to avoid reacting negatively. When you do not feel threatened by another person's opinion or verbal attack, you can look at what is being said without emotional reaction. Arguments aren't necessary. Your self esteem doesn't depend on whether people agree with you or not.

Soft Vision has the same quieting effect on animals as you assess their actions accurately without getting your feelings hurt and without feeling threatened. You will understand animals' communications to you more clearly and you can more effectively communicate your requests to the animal.

Enjoy Soft Vision.

On the Ground

Groundwork is far more than longing a horse to take the edge off his energy levels before you hop into the saddle. Groundwork is a time of honing two-way communication and cooperation.

Approach your horse with a smile and positive body language. Reassure your horse that you care about him and are capable of meeting his needs. Give your horse reason to trust you. Pay full attention to your horse. Avoid talking on the cell phone or chatting with people around you. When you are in the company of a person who is chatting on the phone – you feel ignored. Let your horse know he is worthy of your attention.

While you are simply leading your horse to a different stall or corral, take a moment to assess his physical condition and mood. Listen to what your horse tells to you by his body language. If your horse is uncomfortable or in pain he may limp or flinch when touched.

Feel your horse's back, legs, neck, withers, and belly. Touch your horse everywhere every day. Know how your horse looks and how he feels to your touch so you quickly notice any changes.

Grooming is the ultimate of groundwork. Brushing relaxes your horse and places you in pleasant control of his body. You begin establishing your leadership with a brush, comb and hoof pick as you teach your horse to stand quietly and not resist you. Smiling will help you transmit and teach patience to your horse.

Don't let your horse treat you with disrespect. It may look cute when a horse bumps his head on you grabs your jacket in search of treats hidden in your pocket, but such behavior is disrespectful. If a human pushed you or invaded your space by reaching into your pockets or pulling on your clothes, you would have grounds for assault charges.

Decide where to draw the lines of two-way respect and be certain that you and your horse both understand the limits. Your leadership in the saddle begins with fairness and firmness on the ground.

In the Saddle

Mount up with a smile. Smiling will help you maintain a positive attitude. Remember to breathe. Whenever we are worried we tend to hold our breath, which in turn increases tension in our bodies and causes increased ocular pressure, reducing clear vision. Horses hold their breath when tense or afraid. When the horse feels the rider's deep regular breathing he follows the relaxing example.

Feel yourself melt into the saddle or onto your horse's bare back. Sit relaxed with good posture. Rounding your shoulders in a fetal position may give you the feeling of being in a "safer" position, but it conveys insecurity and fear to your horse and to yourself as well. Smile, breathe, posture.

As you ride, follow good riding rules. Hold your shoulders still, flex in your middle, relax your lower legs keeping good contact with your thighs, toes up heels down, look where you are going and not down at your horse, keep your hands relaxed on the reins and feel your horse's mouth.

Breathing in and out evenly in cadence with your horse's footsteps is a good way to remember to remain relaxed.

Smile with your eyes, gently loving all you see. Smile vision keeps you the present moment instead of letting your mind run away to a past fearful event or rush forward into worry about what might happen.

If you do feel your mind trying to slip back to a past

fearful event or fast forward to a future fear, hum a tune or talk aloud to your horse, or sing a song. Practice using your confidence tools, breathe, relax, smile, and keep your mind in real-time.

Quality and Repetition:

It doesn't require many hours of riding every day to re-learn to ride without fear. If you spend five to ten minutes each day of quality time with your horse on the ground and on his back, you will benefit far more than if you infrequently force yourself to stay in the saddle for long periods of time.

Many thin coats of paint stick far better and are more lasting than thick gobs of paint on a wall. Likewise many short positive sessions on your horse's back are far more healing and encouraging than a long tiring or frustrating session every now and then.

Start small and remain positive. Think of your riding sessions as retraining yourself and as an opportunity to teach your horse and hone his responses to your cues. Explore your relationship with your horse. Communicate. Learn what is important to your horse and assure him that you care. Let it be fun and keep a smile in your eyes and heart.

Ride with leadership. Don't be a pushover. Horses seek leadership and often test the rider by stopping, shaking a head or refusing to obey a cue. This is not a "bad attitude" on the part of the horse, it is the horse making sure that both of you are safe – that the best leader is in charge.

Smile and kindly insist that he do as you ask. When you smile, you relax and dispel negative emotions, allowing you to interact in a positive way and assert your leadership. Your horse will be reassured by your strength and fairness.

Always end an arena training session on a good note. Finish riding when your horse is listening and responding to you well and do remember to praise him. Avoid stopping in the same place every time in the arena. Be as consistent as possible with your cues, but vary your riding patterns so your horse is truly listening to you for guidance and not merely remembering a predictable pattern.

Your horse is a mirror of your mood and attitude. If you are bored, your horse will mirror your boredom. Create interesting riding patterns or obstacles to negotiate. Variety and change will keep your mind in the present moment.

when you have a moment of uncertainty, remember:

Body language
Breathe
Smile
Talk to your horse
Hum or sing a tune

Most importantly:

Live in
Soft -Vision!
☺
Smile softly with your eyes – gently loving all you see!

I know you can be a bombproof human – living in confidence and a place of personal power...and as a bombproof rider, you will put a smile on your horse's face!

In Loving Memory of Amy

Suggested Reading

Rivas, Mim Eichler. *Beautiful Jim Key*. New York, NY :
William Morrow, an Imprint
    of Harper Collins Publishers, 2005.
Fletcher, Carole. *Healed by Horses*. New York, NY : Atria
Press, a trademark of
    Simon and Schuster, Inc., 2005.
Hughes - Calero, Heather. *Woman Between The Wind*.
Cottonwood, AZ : Higher   Consciousness Books, 1990.
Jackson, Jamie. *The Natural Horse*. Harrison, AR : Star
Ridge Publishing, 1997.
Lyons, John. *Lyons on Horses*. New York, NY : Doubleday a
divison of Bantam   Doubleday Dell Publishing Group, Inc.,
1991.

Miller, Robert and Lamb, Richard. *The Revolution in
Horsemanship*. Guilford, CT:
    Lyons Press, an imprint of The Globe Pequot Press,
2005.
Murphy, Dr. Joseph. *Miracles of Your Mind*. New York, NY :
Hay House, Inc.,   1956.
Norris, Desmond. *Horsewatching*. New York, NY : Crown
Publishers, 1988.
Parelli, Pat. *Natural Horse-Man-Ship*. Colorado Springs, CO
: Western Horseman magazine, 1993.
Pony Boy, Gawani. *Horse, Follow Closely*. Irvine, CA : Bow
Tie Press, 1998.
Rashid, Mark. *Considering the Horse*. Boulder CO : Johnson

printing, 1993.

Roberts, Monty. *From My Hand to Yours*. Solvang. CA : Monty and Pat Roberts

Inc., 2002.

Roberts, Monty. *Horse Sense for People*. New York, NY : The Penguin Group   Penguin Putnam Inc., 2000.

Roberts, Monty. *The Man Who Listens to Horses*. New York, NY : Random   House, 1996.

Tellington - Jones, Linda. *The Tellington TTouch*. New York, NY : Viking Penguin,

a division of Penguin Books, 1992.

Tolle, Eckhart. *The Power of Now*. Novato, CA : New World Library, 1999.

Wright, Gordon. *The Cavalry Manual of Horsemanship and Horsemastership*.

Garden City, NY : Doubleday and Company Inc., 1962.

Afterword

Now it's about you! Share your struggle with fear, your insights, victories, defeats – whatever is on your mind, we would love to hear from you – or your horse!

Smiles,
Donna and Truly

Email: djlindahl@gmail.com

CPSIA information can be obtained at www.ICGtesting.com
Printed in the USA
BVOW11s0834151215

430330BV00019B/438/P

9 781477 495056